GUIDEDGUITARCHORD
PRACTICEROUTINES

Master Every Essential Guitar Chord in this Comprehensive 10-Week Course

LEVICLAY

FUNDAMENTALCHANGES

Guided Guitar Chord Practice Routines

Master Every Essential Guitar Chord in this Comprehensive 10-Week Course

ISBN: 978-1-78933-453-1

Published by www.fundamental-changes.com

Copyright © 2024 Levi Clay

Edited by Tim Pettingale

www.fundamental-changes.com

For over 350 free guitar lessons with videos check out:

www.fundamental-changes.com

Join our free Facebook Community of Cool Musicians

www.facebook.com/groups/fundamentalguitar

Tag us for a share on Instagram: **FundamentalChanges**

Cover Image Copyright: Author photo used by permission.

Contents

Introduction

Congratulations on making the step towards taking chords more seriously. I know it sounds hyperbolic, but the day I switched my perspective on music to be more harmony focused, that was the day my musical life changed completely.

We might think of chords as being the domain of the rhythm guitarist (like that's a bad thing!) but the truth is, chords and harmony hold all the power of melody too. Any melody will sound completely different depending on the chord it's being played over, so having an in-depth knowledge of harmony, and understanding how we hear melodies in relation to it, will influence our melodic decisions and make us better soloists.

Most guitar players have a sense of the importance of chords, and over the 20 years I've been teaching, I've often been asked what books I studied to learn all the chords I know. The truth is, I didn't read any! I remember Joe Pass talking about chord books, referring to them as huge compendiums with page after page of chord diagrams that don't help us learn anything. The reality is, trying to learn a thousand chord diagrams is plain silly – and that's before we consider that many voicings just aren't usable in the real world.

So, you won't find page after page of diagrams here. Instead, I'll show you how I worked on harmony. Here you'll find a systematic series of week-long routines, each introducing a new harmonic concept. These routines aren't just about showing you lots of chord shapes to add to your arsenal, they aim to grow your understanding of chord construction, theory, and practical application.

By the end of this book, you should never need another lesson on chords. You'll have all the tools you need to be able to build any chord you like and find your own voicings.

That said, chords are built from scales, so having a solid understanding of scales is going to be essential to your progress in this pursuit. This book is number two in a series, so I'll assume (or at least hope) that you've already worked through the first book, *Guided Guitar Scale Practice Routines*.

The routines contained here might feel like a lot of work at first, but remember, this is all about a complete shift in perspective – one that will revolutionise your playing. If you feel like you're wading through mud at first, that's completely normal. You are reprogramming the way you think. We're not just buying a house here, we're learning how to think like architects and engineers!

But I promise you it'll be worth it. So let's get on with it.

Levi

How To Use This Book

I've gone out of my way to make the books in my guided practice series different from every guitar book you've read before, and this one is no different.

Not only is there a full description of each exercise and downloadable audio for every example, there's also an additional full-length recording of each entire routine, with all the repeats, and with me talking you through it as we play it together. If you prepare yourself to play these full routines with me every day, I guarantee you will see growth.

There are only three rules for how to use this book…

First, learn the material, then practice the routines!

Although the routines are designed to each span one week, it's likely that they'll take longer. I always talk about the difference between learning and practice. We learn a thing, then we practice it. If you already know all the material, then you can jump straight into practicing it and be done in a week. However, if you're learning things that are new to you, that information must be solidly in place before you leap into the practice routine.

Don't feel the need to rush, otherwise you'll get discouraged. Take a week or two just to learn the exercises if you need. Rushing will just lead to roadblocks in your playing later. There's a lot of stuff here, so take your time with it.

Second, while this book will arm you with every concept you'll ever need to master chords, it's not possible to notate every possible permutation of each exercise in every key. We didn't want to publish an intimidating 750-page book. Talk about off-putting! I'll hold your hand for the journey but there will come a point where you'll need to take a chord type you've learned and apply the principles of practice for yourself. The more you put in, the more you'll get out.

Lastly, let me briefly mention songs too. We have to remember that playing music is ultimately about playing songs. There are a ton of exercises here that are applied to various chord progressions, but nothing beats using the chords/concepts in this book by applying them to real songs that you know or want to learn.

My main gig is in the Soul genre, so I'm deep into that traditional RnB, Blues and Gospel sound – but you can apply these ideas to whatever style is your bag. Be sure to do that, because that's what's going to make you a real musician – someone who can get up and play songs and make them sound good.

That's about it, so let's start our routines!

Get the Audio

The audio files for this book are available to download for free from **www.fundamental-changes.com.**

The link is in the top right-hand corner. Click on the "Guitar" link then simply select this book title from the drop-down menu and follow the instructions to get the audio.

We recommend that you download the files directly to your computer, not to your tablet, and extract them there before adding them to your media library.

For over 350 free guitar lessons with videos check out:

www.fundamental-changes.com

Join our free Facebook Community of Cool Musicians

www.facebook.com/groups/fundamentalguitar

Tag us for a share on Instagram: FundamentalChanges

Routine One – Chord Grips

In this first chapter, I want to address what I call *chord grips.* The guitar is an interesting instrument because it combines the ability to play chords like a piano with portability. It's quite unique in this respect, which is why it has a long history of being the go-to tool for singer-songwriters.

Above all other instruments, the guitar is also incredibly shaped based. I've met countless guitarists who can play chords that they can't name. Typically, they have learned a bunch of open chords, maybe a few barre chords, then they just move them around to get the sound they want. That doesn't happen with pianists. That's not to say I think it's wrong, though. In fact, I think it's awesome. It means we're able to learn chords on the guitar quickly, whereas on the piano we have to learn the notes that go into a chord before we can play it.

I wanted to write this book in a way that celebrates the accessibility of the guitar, so we're going to start there. We're going to use the familiar open chord shapes as reference points from which we'll build and explore. Don't worry, we'll learn the theory that backs up every idea too, but having clear reference points from which we can work on harmony will give our practice some real focus.

You may have heard these open chords affectionally referred to as "cowboy chords". If you know these chords and own a capo, then you'll be able to strum a lifetime of songs around the campfire! You won't be thinking about issues like chord construction, key signatures or harmony theory, but at least you'll have a selection of grips your hand can effortlessly jump to.

The five most important open chords are E major, D major, C major, A major, and G major.

To warm up, we're going to cycle through them, just thinking of them as physical grips and focusing on achieving good fretting technique and clean execution.

Example 1a:

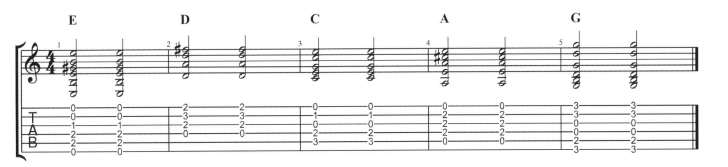

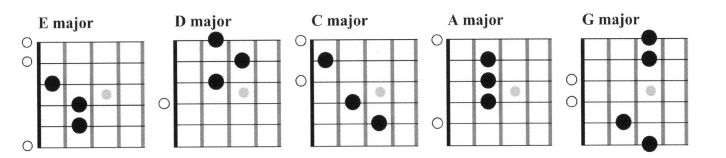

Some of you may have made the connection to the CAGED system (or EDCAG as I laid it out). We'll delve deeper into that soon, but for now we're making sure we have the most common chord grips under our hands.

Moving on, what about open position minor chords?

Example 1b:

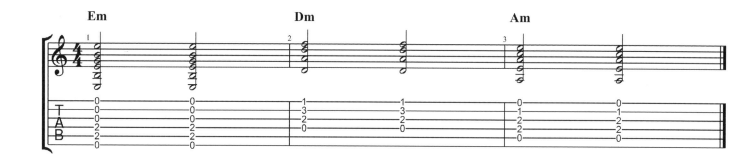

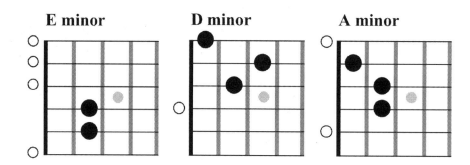

You'll notice there's no open C minor or G minor. These are theoretically possible to play, but hard work on the hand, so they are never played in the real world.

Of course, there are lots more open chords to learn – 7th chords, inversions, suspended chords, slash chords and more – but they are all based on the five chords in Example 1a. For example:

Example 1c:

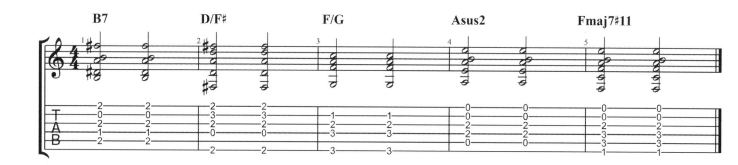

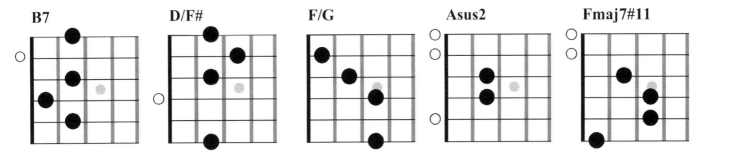

How many singer-songwriters have managed to write entire libraries of material using just three of these basic chords? The secret is making sure we can transition effortlessly between the common chord grips, as in the next example.

Example 1d:

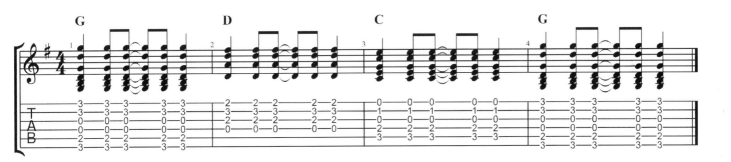

The next step in developing the basic open shapes is turning them into their barred forms. The most commonly used is the E major chord, moved up the neck one fret at a time. For that reason, we call this the "E shape".

Example 1e:

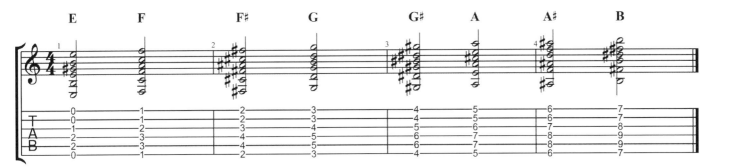

We can move each open chord in the same way. Here's the A shape moved up the neck. Notice that I don't try to get the note on the high E string when barring. Instead, I use the ring finger to barre the D, G, and B strings, but I know that top note could be there if I wanted.

Example 1f:

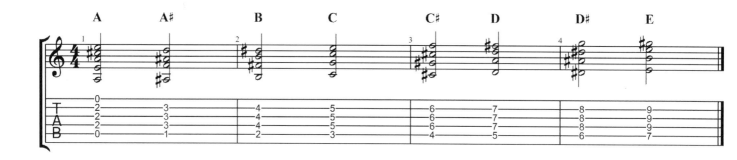

Next, here's the C shape. This one in incredibly important and is the shape every one of my new students struggles with. Sort it out!

Example 1g:

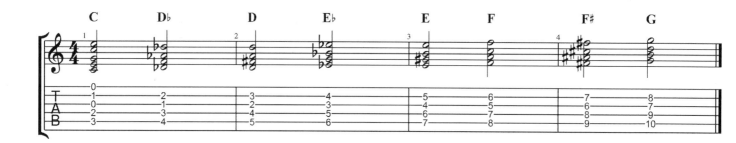

When it comes to moveable D and G shapes, they are possible, but I can honestly say the last time I played these was when I was recording the audio for a different book. There's a difference between what's possible and what's practical in the real world. I always veer towards the pragmatic! Try them anyway.

Example 1h:

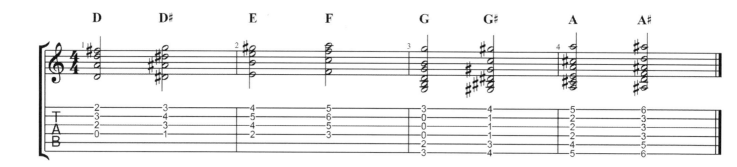

So the most important of our shapes are the E, A, and C shapes. The following exercise cycles through three G major chord voicings, first in the E shape, then the C shape, then the A shape.

When doing this, it's incredibly important to focus on one thing only: the root note on the E or A string. That's all I'm seeing. I look for that note, then I put the correct chord grip on top of it.

Example 1i:

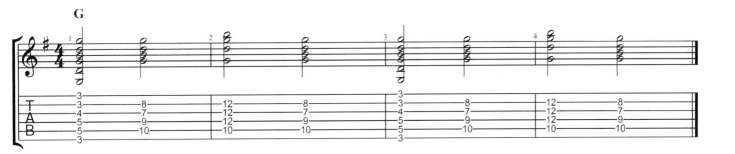

Here's the same idea applied to a C major chord. Focus on the C root note on the 3rd fret of the A string, then the 8th fret of the low E, jumping up to the 15th fret on the A string for the higher octave.

Example 1j:

When we think like this, we can identify the root note movements for a progression like E – G#m – A – B and plug chord grips on top of them. Here's that progression using E shape chords, but on the repeat we're throwing in a C shape for the E major, just to mix things up.

Example 1k:

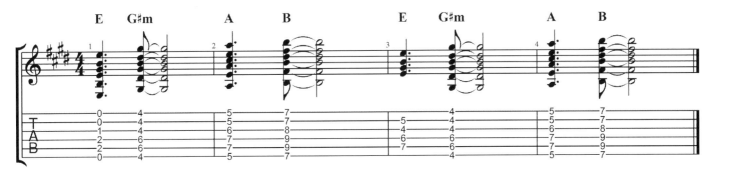

I made a big deal in my previous book about the use of the Circle of 5ths as a tool for practicing in twelve keys, and nowhere is that more useful that here.

As a reminder, starting on C, the Circle of 5ths pattern is:

C – F – Bb – Eb – Ab – Db – Gb – B – E – A – D – G – C

Apply that to the fretboard using our E, A, and C grips, and we have the following

Example 1l:

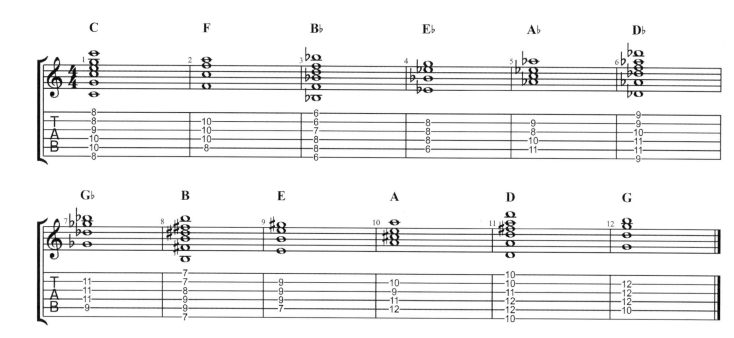

There are a lot of ways we could play through this progression. Just focus on looking for the root note of each chord on the E or A string, then apply the chord grip that fits on that root note. Here's a pathway starting down in the A shape.

Example 1m:

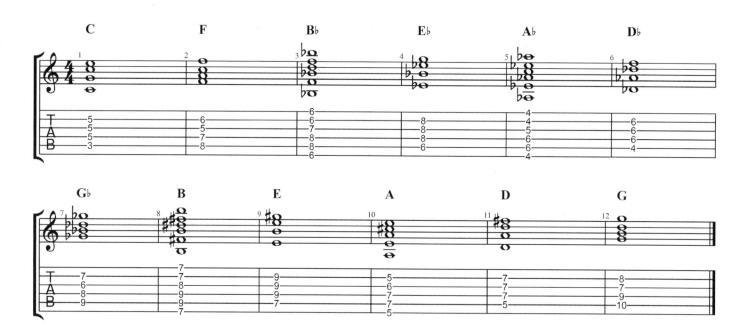

For one final example, we could move through our three chord grips on each chord to keep us on our toes, always looking for the next chord change while developing the fretboard relationship between different voicings of the same chord.

Example 1n:

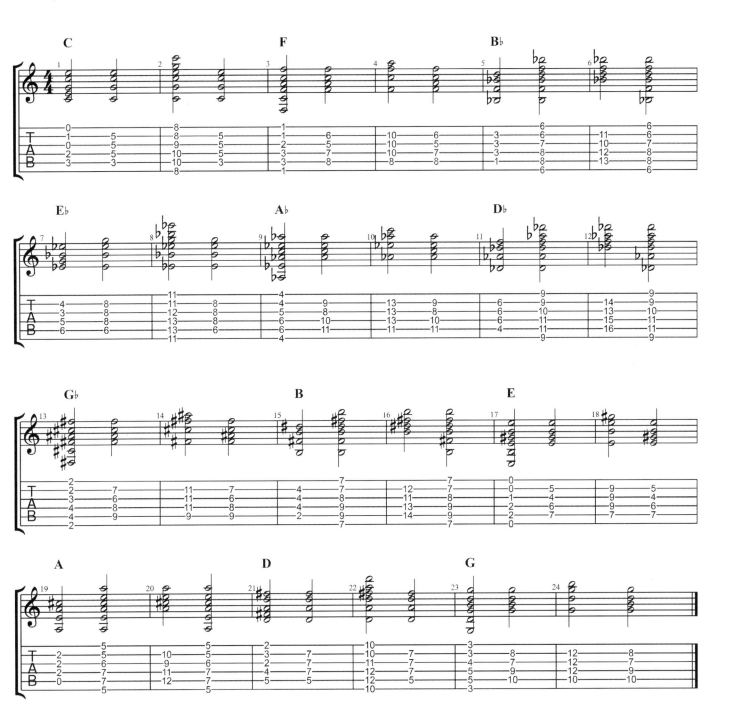

Spend some time getting used to these shapes because we're going to be using them as visualisation tools to help focus our study of chord construction.

See you there!

Routine Two – Major Triad Workout

Now we're going to start thinking about chords from the perspective of chord theory and construction. Chords are built from the notes of scales, so a sound knowledge of scales is essential. In my guided scale practice book, I placed huge emphasis on knowing your intervals, because that's how we hear notes – the distance between the note we're playing and the root note of the scale. It's that interval relationship that gives each note its emotional impact.

Our Western system of harmony is based on the principle of *tertian* harmony. In other words, we form chords by stacking them in 3rds. Let's take the C Major scale (C D E F G A B C). If we take the first note, then a note a 3rd higher, then a note another 3rd higher, that gives us C, E, and G. Together they form a C major triad – the tonic chord of the scale.

Let's apply that to the guitar. Here is the C Major scale played on the A string, followed by the notes of the triad (the 1st, 3rd and 5th degrees of the scale).

Example 2a:

So, the root, 3rd and 5th of the major scale are the ingredients of a major triad. Knowing those intervals feels much more useful than trying to remember the pitches of each note. And the formula is the same whatever key you happen to be playing in.

Sticking with C major (C E G), it doesn't matter where those notes are played, or in what order (C doesn't have to be the lowest note), they will always spell a C major triad. And there are lots of ways we can play those three notes on guitar. Here's a small selection of them:

Example 2b:

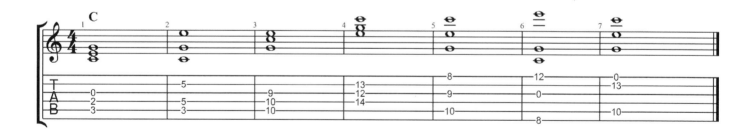

It wouldn't be practical to memorise every possible triad voicing that can be played on guitar. Instead, we need a system of organisation to help compartmentalise different areas of the fretboard. Fortunately, we've already done the bulk of the work by learning our E, A, and C grips. Here is an easy way to break down those shapes into triads.

It's possible to play C major in the C shape utilising every string, as in bar one of Example 2c. Then, if we break that big shape down into several smaller shapes, each one arranged on three adjacent strings, we get this:

Example 2c:

Let's take a look at what just happened.

Remember that it's a C major triad (C E G), even if the notes appear in a different order. On the top three strings we have the notes G, C, E, low to high. On the next string set we have E, G, C. Then we have C, E, G, and finally G, C, E on the bottom three strings.

The thing to notice about this pattern is that each new triad is formed by taking the highest note of the previous one and moving it to the bottom.

We took the high E note from the triad on the top three strings, and moved it to the bottom of the triad on the next string set. Then we took the high C note from that triad and moved it to the bottom of the next one, and so on.

We call these *closed voiced* triads. This means that all the notes in the chord are arranged as close together as possible (usually on adjacent strings), fit within an octave, and are stacked in 3rds.

If we do the same with the A shape, we get the following.

Example 2d:

The main mistake students tend to make when working on this is not grasping the idea of moving from one triad to the next by taking the *top note* and moving it to the *bottom*.

For example, after playing the second triad in bar two above, arranged on the D, G and B strings, they will just move every note across a string at the 5th fret. But this means they're now playing the notes C, G, C and it's no longer a triad. Instead, the E note on top of that shape needs relocating to the 7th fret of the A string. It's crucial to get into our heads this idea of taking the top note and moving it to the bottom!

Let's do the same with the E shape, focusing on the top note moving to the bottom each time.

Example 2e:

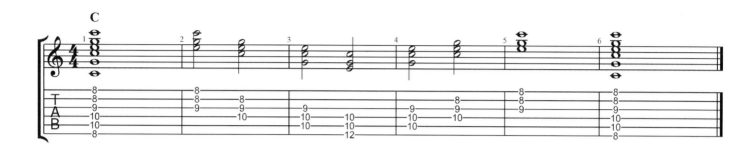

If we put all of this into diagram form, it immediately becomes clear how the major triads lay out across the neck in three distinct areas. I call them the A, E, and C shapes, because I visualise them around those CAGED patterns. These are my "master patterns".

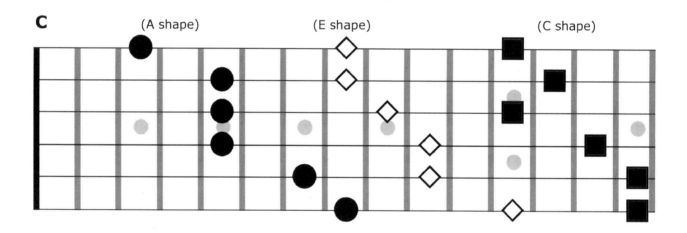

The goal we are working towards is to effortlessly play triads across all string sets in any key – and to be able to do so because we can *see* those bigger barre forms. Let's switch to a G major triad. Think about the larger barre shapes and pick out the closed voiced triads.

Example 2f:

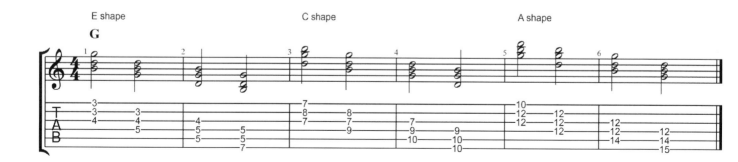

I call this approach *vertical* because we're moving triads across the strings in a single area of the fretboard. But we can also take a *horizontal* approach, where we play along the length of the neck.

In Example 2g, we take the first E shape G major triad and move it on the same strings to the C shape, then the A shape. Then we play the E shape again in the higher octave before descending. This tests our ability to immediately visualise the big barre forms in each zone of the neck, while picking out the smaller triads.

Then we move to the E shape G major triad voiced on the D, G and B strings, repeat the process, and so on.

Example 2g:

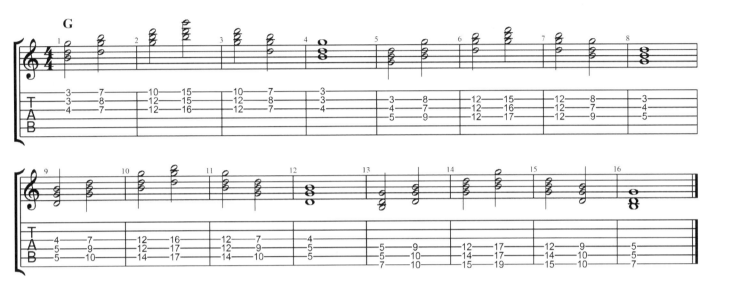

There are lots of ways to practice these three positions, and I'm a firm believer in the idea that the more we stress our brains in the practice room, the more results we'll see. So, I like to combine horizontal and vertical approaches to test myself.

In the following example, we start with a G major triad on the low strings. To move to the next voicing, we have two choices:

Vertical – stay in position and change string set.

Horizontal – change position using the same string set.

The goal we're working towards is to always be able to *see* these two options, so that we can choose one and, when we move to it, visualise the *next* two options. This exercise isn't easy!

Example 2h:

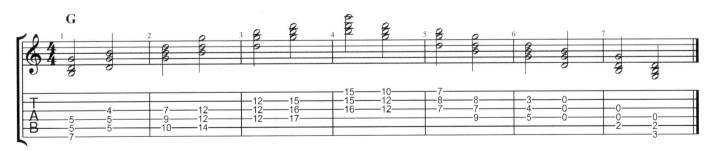

We can do this with any major triad. The key is visualising our three larger "master patterns", so we can confidently pick out the smaller, closed voiced triads. Here's the same idea outlining a C major chord.

Example 2i:

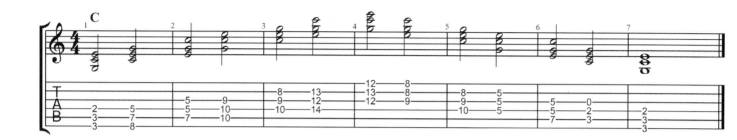

At this stage, we're still mostly thinking about closed voiced triads as shapes. We'll focus much more on their intervals in next week's routine. But first, we have to learn to confidently see them.

Let's work around the Circle of 4ths this time and only play triads on the D, G, B string set. It's the same idea as the previous routine: we're looking for the big barre chord, then playing a smaller triad within it.

Example 2j:

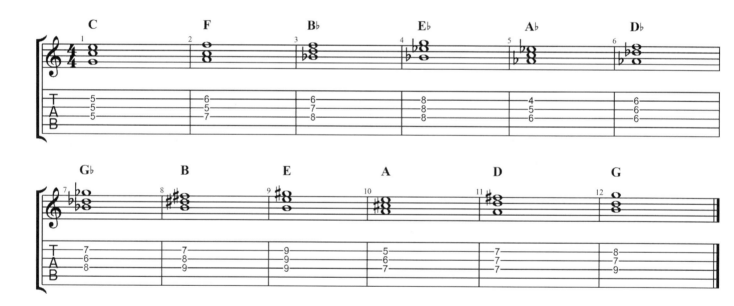

To keep us on our toes, let's repeat that but play two triads in horizontal fashion for each chord.

Example 2k:

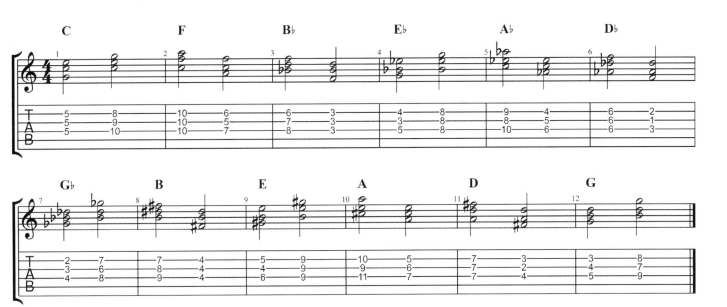

You could (and should!) be working on this in your own practice times, aiming to do the same thing on different string sets – like this example, where we play only the top three strings.

Example 2l:

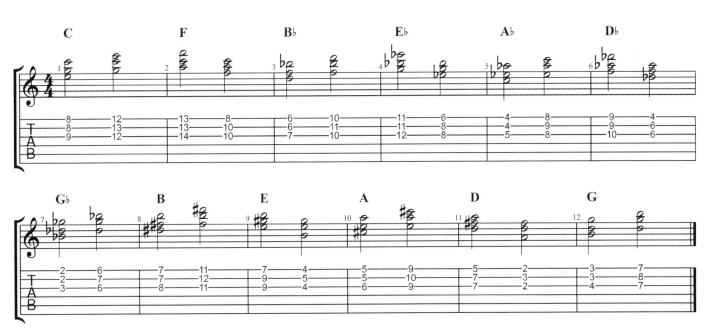

Now I want you to do that on all string sets, breaking them up horizontally and vertically! Challenge yourself. Stress your brain!

Thankfully, you're not likely to have to do anything as stressful as this in real world music, so now I want to look at some practical chord progressions. To begin with, I–IV–V patterns.

If that terminology is new to you, let's quickly decode it.

In a major key (let's take C Major), the chords built on the 1st, 4th and 5th scale degrees are all major chords. Every chord in a key is assigned a Roman numeral, hence we have a I–IV–V sequence (1 4 5). In C Major those chords are C, F and G.

We can learn the pattern of a sequence like this. If you know where your I chord is located, the IV will always be in the same place in relation to it, as will the V chord.

Example 2m:

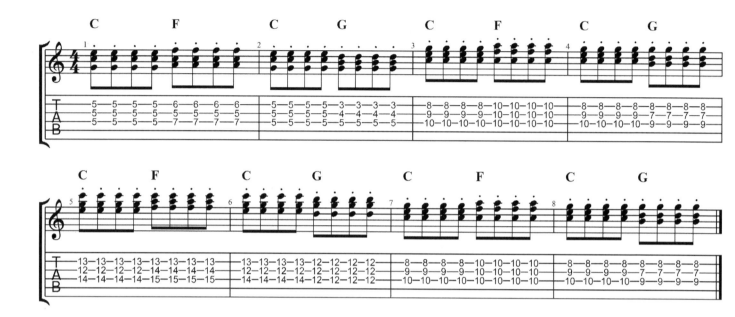

Here's the same idea played on the A, D, G string set.

Example 2n:

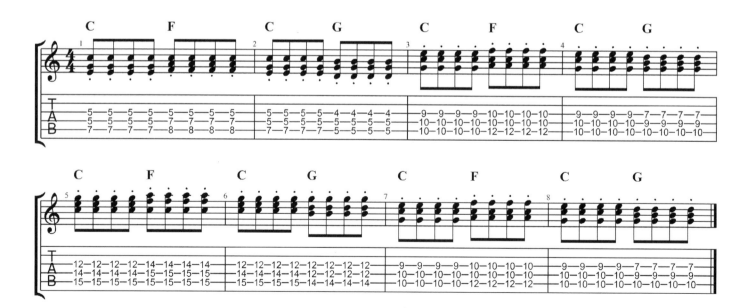

The relationship between a major chord and a chord a 4th higher can be called a "I–IV move". I use this idea all the time to add a little colour to a major chord. So, in the following example, we play C *and* F triads over a C major harmony. We do the same for the F major chord, using F and Bb triads, and the same for G major, using G and C triads. You can create an instant riff with this idea.

Example 2o:

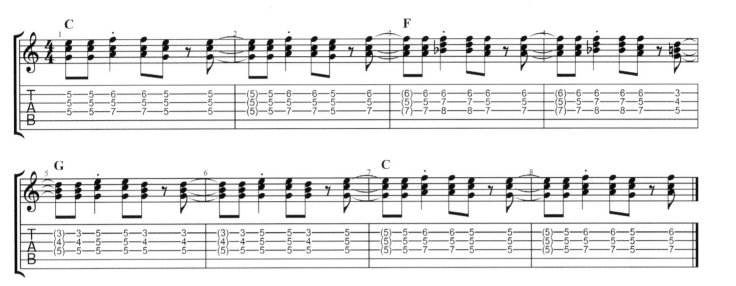

Here's the same I–IV movement on the top strings, using a slightly different rhythmic idea.

Example 2p:

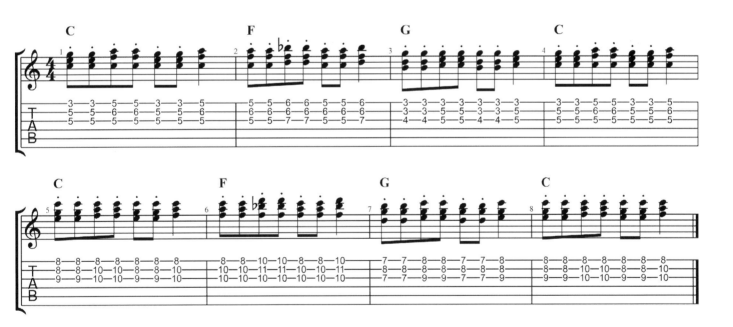

As we continue to study, you'll notice that major triads come up time and again. Not just on the I, IV and V chords in a key, but on lots of others. So, don't underestimate the importance of this week's routine. Major triads are incredibly versatile and we need to know their voicings inside out, without hesitation, in any key.

Routine Three – Minor Triads & Beyond

Everything we've done so far can be repeated with the major scale's sibling, the natural minor scale.

C Natural Minor has the notes C D Eb F G Ab Bb C

Using the principle of tertian harmony we can take the first note, skip the next, then skip another note, and we have C, Eb, G – a C minor triad.

This the principal triad in the minor scale and it's the pepper to the major triad's salt.

Example 3a:

The important thing to spot here is that the difference between a major triad and a minor triad is just one note – the b3. We can take *any* major triad, lower its 3rd to a b3, and we'll have a minor triad.

In order to be able to do this effortlessly, we need to know where the 3rd is located in any of our major triad voicings. At this point, we shift away from *shapes* and begin to think much more about *intervals*.

In our chord grips routine, we put a lot of emphasis on finding the root note on the E and A strings. This is a great starting point, because if we can confidently see the root note, we can work out where other intervals are located. I always apply my "If this, therefore this" principle when learning. In other words, if we know one thing, we can use it to deduce another thing.

You're probably very proficient in locating root notes on the E and A strings, but we need to know where all the root notes are to apply this principle. So, take another look at the E, C and A shape major barre chords. Start by looking at the root notes on the E and A strings, then focus on learning the octave patterns to locate the higher root notes.

E shape

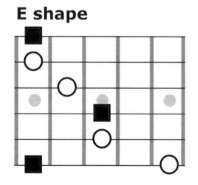

C shape

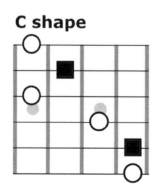

A shape

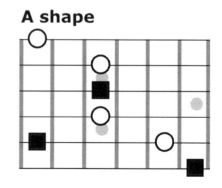

Practice locating all the root notes until you can drop on them at will in all three shapes. It might take a little while to commit to memory, but it's an important step. If we know where the root notes are, we can use them to work out where the 3rd interval is located.

Here's the key: if you know where the root note is, the next note up will *always* be the 3rd.

Let's work through this using a G major chord (G B D). In bar one of Example 3b, we play a G major triad on the top three strings. We know from studying the E shape diagram that the root is located on the D string, below this voicing. Therefore, we know that the note on the G string must be the 3rd. We can then flatten this note to a b3 (Bb) to make a G minor triad.

In bar two, we move onto the next string set. The G root is there on the D string, and we know that the note above it on the G string is the 3rd, which we flatten to make G minor.

The 3rd is still located on the G string when we move down to the next string set.

Finally, when we're on the lowest string set, we're not using the G string anymore, so the 3rd must be located on a new string. In this instance, it's the Bb note on the E string, 6th fret.

Example 3b:

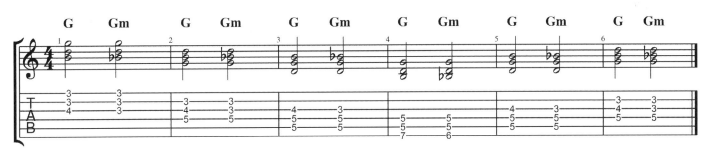

Now let's apply this idea to the C shape.

Example 3c:

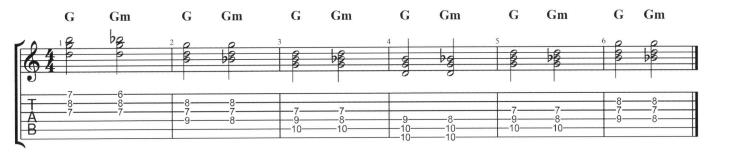

23

And the A shape.

Example 3d:

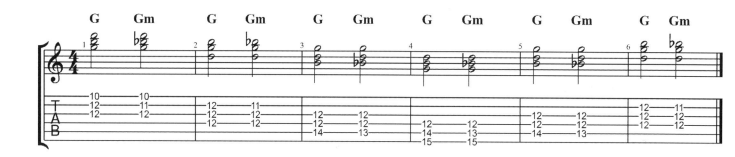

Converting major triads into minor triads is important interval training for us, but once we know this, we can begin drilling minor triads in their own right, without needing to play the major triad first. The diagram below shows all three large minor barre shapes at a glance.

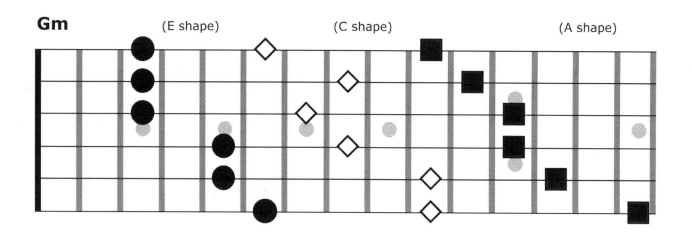

Here are the smaller G minor triads contained within the large shapes, played consecutively.

Example 3e:

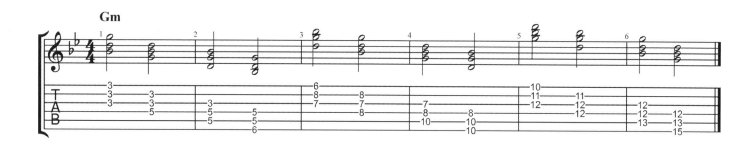

The obvious next step is to be able to do this in any key. Here we're playing C minor triads.

Example 3f:

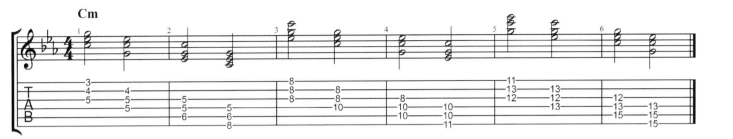

Let's stay with C minor but combine vertical and horizonal approaches.

Example 3g:

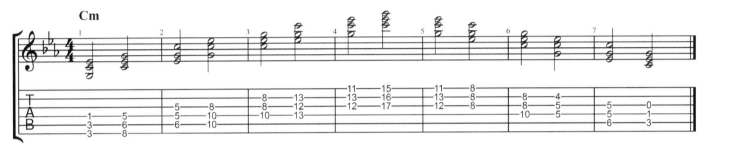

Minor chords are also found in the major scale, not just the minor scale. Using the C Major scale (C D E F G A B C) we built a major triad from the root note (C E G). If we build a triad from the 2nd, we get a D minor triad (D F A). The second chord in a major key is always a minor triad.

A common chord move that I use all the time over a major chord is to combine these major and minor triads. So, over a C major chord, I'll combine C major and D minor triads. This works, even though the harmony stays on C.

Example 3h:

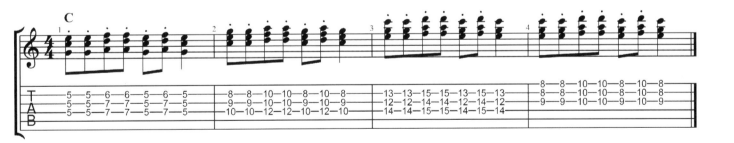

In the previous example, we played each measure on the same string set, but we could also combine string sets in a vertical fashion, as shown in the following idea that works over C and F chords. This means we're playing C major and D minor triads over C, and F major and G minor triads over F.

Example 3i:

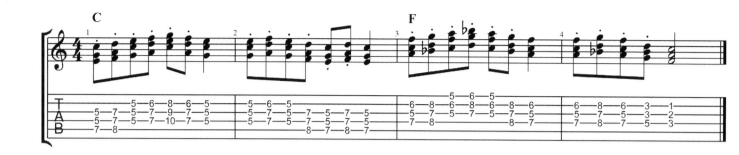

Now let's look at some chord progressions that combine major and minor triads to give ourselves some vehicles to practice with.

First up, let's play a I–vi–ii–IV chord progression. This comes up in tons of songs, such as Taylor Swift's *Blank Space*. (Notice that the Roman numeral system uses lower case letters for minor chords and upper case for major).

In the key of C Major, the I–vi–ii–IV is C major, A minor, D minor, F major. Here are a few ways I might voice that on the fretboard. Make sure you can visualise the bigger shapes of each triad!

Example 3j:

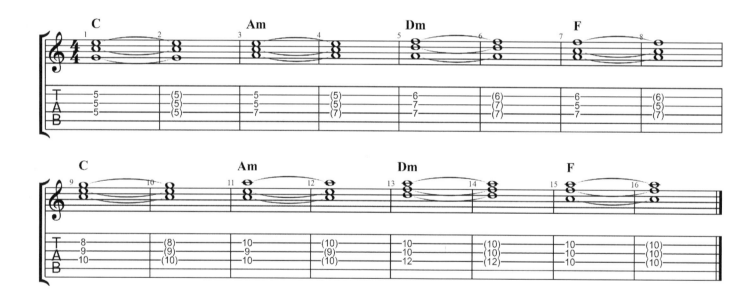

We can achieve a lot using triads like this. For example, if we add some volume swells using a pedal or the volume knob, and add a bit of delay, we can create some nice textures.

Example 3k:

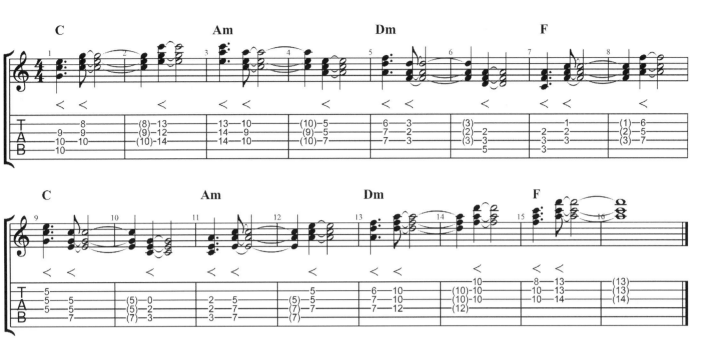

The previous example is a great approach to take if you want to simulate the sound of strings. If you're playing a tune like *Freebird* by Lynyrd Skynyrd, and don't have an organ player, you can replicate that sound too using triads. Here, we play through the progression twice on the D, G, B strings, then twice on the A, D, G string set. Of course, you can (and should) come up with different places to play this every time you practice.

Example 3l:

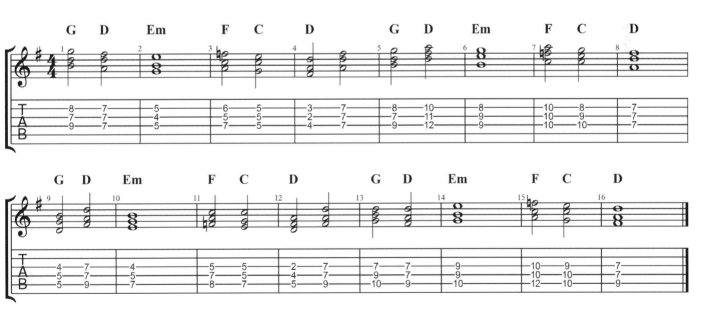

Before we conclude this routine, I want to briefly introduce two more triads to complete our musical palette. We've covered…

- Major – 1 3 5

- Minor – 1 b3 5

But from those two triads we can also make:

- Diminished – 1 b3 b5

- Augmented – 1 3 #5

The diminished triad is a minor triad with a flattened (diminished) 5th. Here's an example where we play minor triads from the E shape of G minor, followed by G diminished triads. This allows us to focus on where that b5 is located.

Example 3m:

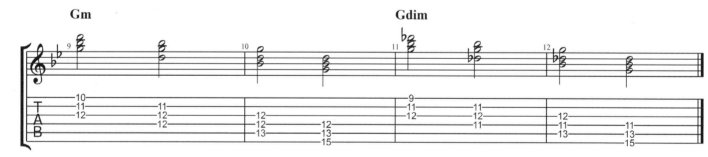

The augmented triad is a major triad with a raised (augmented) 5th. Play the full major triads, then switch to augmented to see where the #5 sits.

Example 3n:

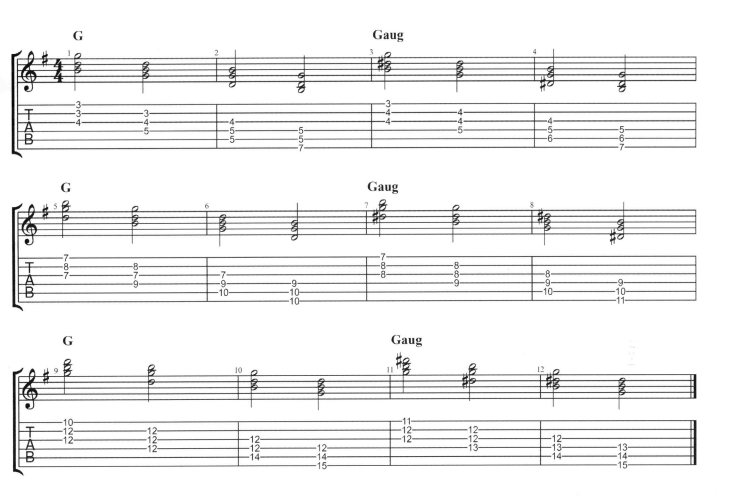

The augmented triad is an interesting sound because it doesn't appear in the major scale. Plus, all the notes in the augmented triad are a major 3rd away from each other, so it's symmetrical. This becomes even more apparent when we play it in horizontal form. Each of the three triads on any given string set are the same!

Example 3o:

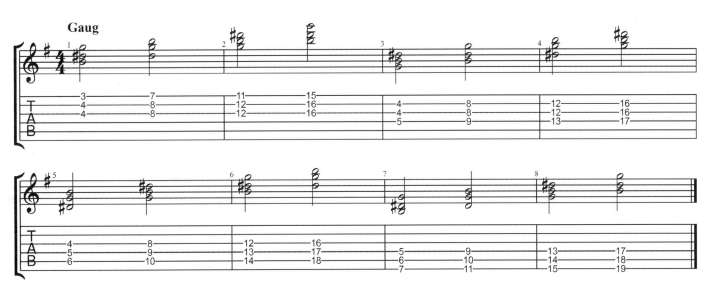

For one final exercise, I'd like to present my patented (it's not patented!) "hardest triad exercise in existence". This entails putting all twelve major, minor, diminished and augmented triads into a random list generator to randomise the order. For a non-techie approach, you could do the same using cue cards with chord names written on them, shuffled into a random order.

The result is a chaotic series of 48 chords of different types. Now we pick an area of the neck and work on playing the triads in the order presented. Here's one randomly generated sequence!

Ab, F#aug, Adim, Bbdim, A, G, Fdim, Eb, Bbaug, Fm, Dbdim, Ebaug, Gdim, F#m, Abdim, Caug, Eaug, Dm, Abm, Gm, Ebm, B, Em, Daug, F, Dbm, Bm, F#dim, Baug, D, Cm, Db, Ddim, Aaug, Ebdim, C, Gaug, Am, Bb, Edim, Bbm, Cdim, Faug, Bdim, Dbaug, E, Abaug, F#.

It's impossible to remember all of that, so we have to work on being able to read it. The result might look something like this.

Example 3p:

30

Randomising those triads wasn't particularly musical, but it's the kill or cure approach to knowing your triads inside out. If you're still with me, well done, because that one was nuts! There's nothing else in this book that's harder or as unmusical, but sometimes you just have to take your medicine. Take some time with this exercise and try your own randomised sequences. In the next routine we're going to focus on chord scales. See you there!

Routine Four – Chord Scales

We've spent three weeks working on chord construction and now have the knowledge to build all the essential triads we're likely to come up against. Next, I want us to look at the relationships between chords and how they work with each other. We'll do this by looking at diatonic chord scales.

Not only will this give you a deeper understanding of which chords work well together, it's a great way of making sure you know all the chords we've already looked at.

In last week's routine, I mentioned the first two chords that can be built from the C Major scale. If we harmonise every note of C Major, then we get the following "chord scale".

C Major (C D E F G A B C) gives us:

C E G – C major (I)

D F A – D minor (ii)

E G B – E minor (iii)

F A C – F major (IV)

G B D – G major (V)

A C E – A minor (vi)

B D F – B diminished (vii)

This pattern of chords is consistent for *every* major scale. Chords I, IV and V are always major. Chords ii, iii and vi are always minor, and chord vii is always diminished.

Let's look at this on the fretboard. Here we have a C Major chord scale played on the A, D, G strings. After playing the C major triad, I say to myself, "Chord ii is minor" as I move up to D minor. Then I say, "Chord iii is minor" as I move to E minor, and so on. Speaking it out helps us to memorise the chord types, understand their position in the scale, and know what we're looking for next.

Example 4a:

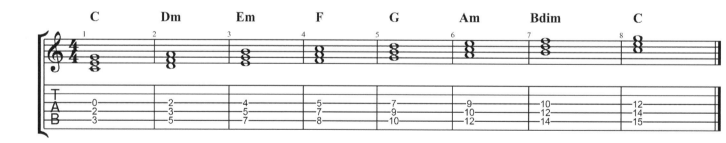

We can do this on any string set. Here's the same exercise on the D, G, B strings.

Example 4b:

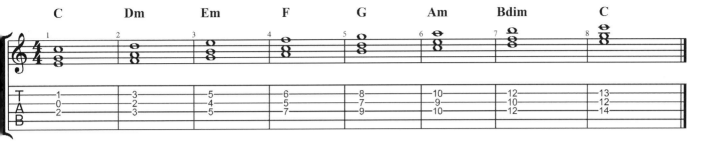

And on the G, B, E string set.

Example 4c:

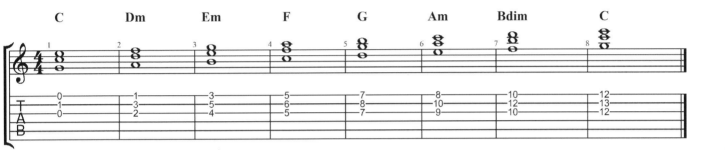

Now let's change key to F Major (F G A Bb C D E F) and play the chord scale starting in the E shape. This time we're playing all four triads in position for each chord.

Example 4d:

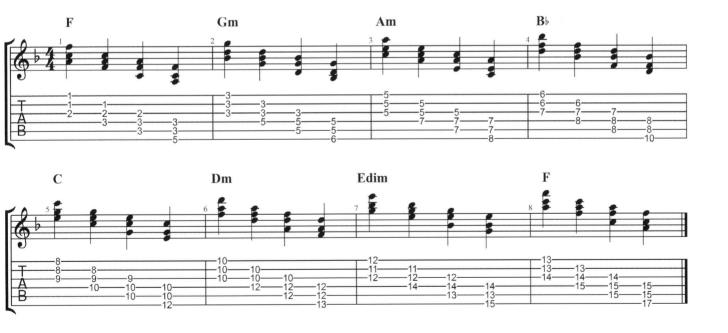

Let's change again. Here's a Bb Major (Bb C D Eb F G A Bb) chord scale starting in the A shape.

Example 4e:

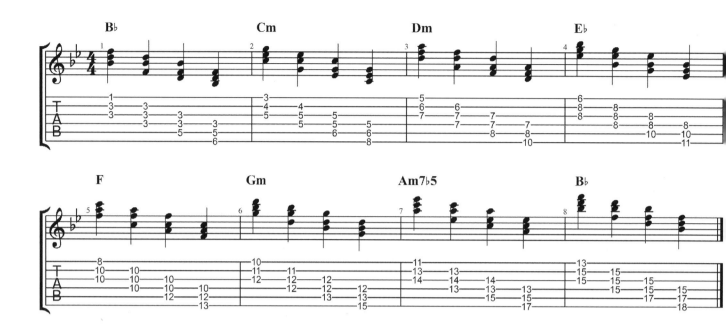

Getting good at this just means picking different keys and getting it done. Here's an E Major chord scale on the top strings starting in the C shape.

Example 4f:

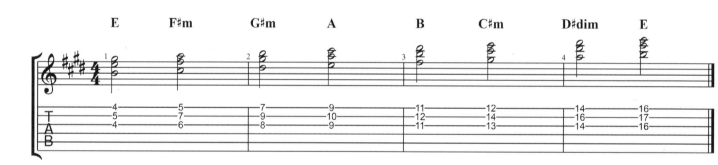

The challenge when playing these chord scales is that panic often sets in when we reach the diminished triad. We can work on hearing/seeing the diminished triad better by starting high and descending. Here's an E Major chord scale descending, starting in the E shape, and moving through three different string sets.

Example 4g:

Let's go back to the C Major scale. A good exercise to practice our triads is to play them ascending and descending. Here, we play a C Major chord scale on the top string set using the C shape.

Example 4h:

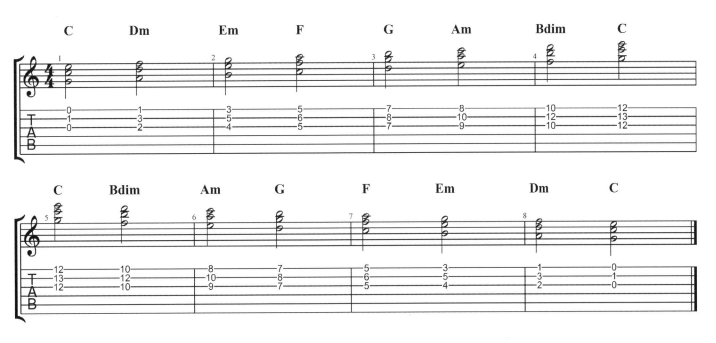

I like to take this idea to the extreme by ascending the scale on one string set, descending on the set below, ascending on the set below that, and then descending on the final set!

Example 4i:

Then, we can take this idea around the Cycle of 4ths by moving to F Major in the E shape.

Example 4j:

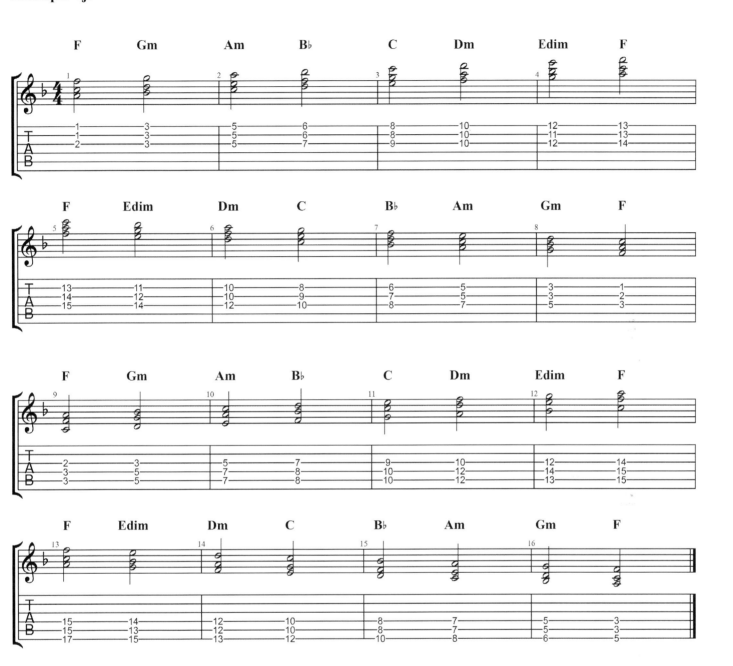

And continue round the Circle to Bb using the A shape.

Example 4k:

For the sake of space, I'm not going to write out all twelve keys using three triad shapes – that would eat up about 20 pages. But, each time you sit down to work on this concept, add a new key and a new position.

For completeness, I want to use the last part of this routine to give you a crash course in chord scales that are not derived from the major scale. There are three useful ones – all of them minor.

C Natural Minor – C D Eb F G Ab Bb C

C Harmonic Minor – C D Eb F G Ab B C

C Melodic Minor – C D Eb F G A B C

The natural minor scale has a symbiotic relationship with the major scale. It contains the same notes, just from a different starting point, so it's known as the *relative minor scale*. You locate the relative minor by going to the 6th degree of the major scale, so in the key of C Major, the relative minor is A Minor.

If we're talking about the C Natural Minor, that shares notes with Eb Major. (C minor is chord vi in the key of Eb Major). Here it is played as a chord scale.

Example 4l:

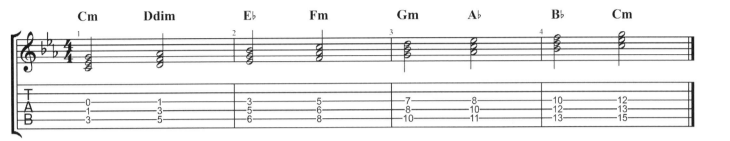

As an aside, in Roman numerals, some might describe this chord scale as i, ii, iii, etc. That's not wrong, but it makes more sense to learn it as:

i – iidim – bIII – iv – v – bVI – bVII – i

Although initially this might seem more complicated, it accurately describes what each chords is. In a minor key we have a ii diminished chord; we have a major chord built on the b3 of the scale; a major chord on the b7, and so on.

These are true-to-life chord functions. When you see a chord progression that mixes chords from both major and minor keys, using this naming convention will help you to identify them. For example, the progression…

C – Am – Bb – Dm – C

…can be described as I–vi–bVII–ii–I.

Example 4m:

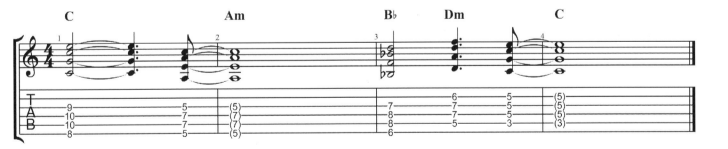

Or, C – G – Ab – Bb – C, would be:

I–V–bVI–bVII–I.

Example 4n:

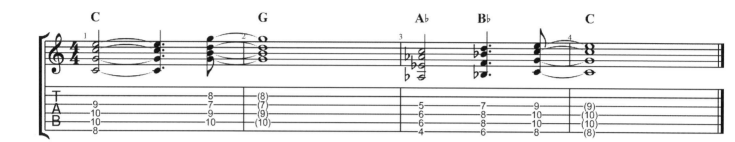

Or, C – Em – F – Fm – C, would be:

I–iii–IV–iv–I.

Example 4o:

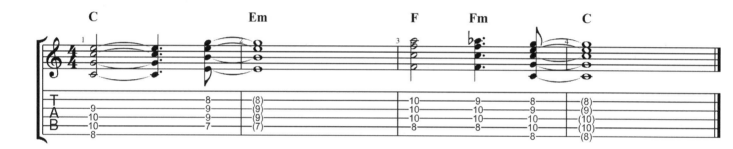

All of the above chord progressions were in the key of C Major, but we borrowed commonly used chords from the key of C Minor.

Technically, the idea of borrowing chords from another key/scale is called *modal interchange*, but 100s of tunes use this idea, and I'm sure the composers weren't led by theory – they just heard a cool sound they liked! However, using the correct Roman numerals to label them is a big help.

Moving on to the C Harmonic Minor scale, harmonising the scale gives us this set of chord designations:

i – iidim – bIII+ – iv – V – bVI – viidim – i

This scale contains two diminished triads and even an augmented triad (the + sign means #5). Let's play through the triads.

Example 4p:

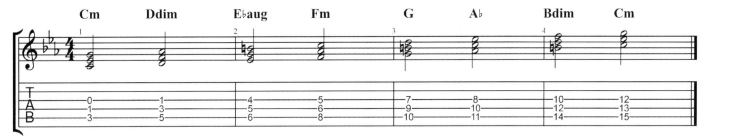

Finally, the C Melodic Minor scale gives us:

i – ii – bIII+ – IV – V – vidim – viidim – i

This scale also has two diminished triads and an augmented triad, but in different places.

Example 4q:

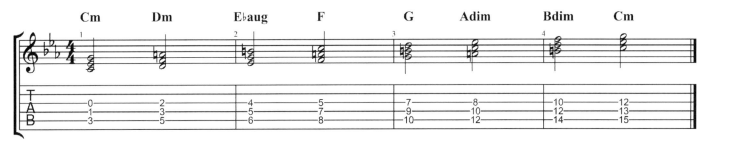

Many tunes have been written based on harmonic minor scale progressions, or by blending harmonic and natural minor scales. *Paint it Black* by the Rolling Stones, *Bury a Friend* by Billie Eilish, *Infinity on High* by Fall Out Boy, and *I Should Have Known Better* by the Beatles are all examples. The same is true of the melodic minor, with tunes like *Yesterday* by the Beatles and more.

This means it's worth your while exploring these scales in more depth. We've played them here only on the A, D, G string set, using just the C shape. You can, of course, work on them in all twelve keys, on all four string sets, using all three shapes! That's a LOT of work, but it'll keep your practice times fresh. Remember, it's not a race, and one day you'll just know all this stuff.

Until next time, get practicing!

Routine Five – Open Voiced Triads & Inversions

So far, all of the chord voicings we've played have been "closed voiced" triads. In other words, the notes are located as close together as possible, and they fit within the span of an octave. Closed voicings have a focused sound and are "dense" compared with the other voicing options we have at our disposal.

In this chapter we're going to expand our triads into *open* voicings. As the name suggests, an open voicing is one that is spread out and spans more than an octave. They sound much more spacious and delicate than their closed counterparts.

Thankfully, they are pretty easy to conceptualise. The diagram below shows a closed voiced C major triad (left) with the root note on the D string (C E G). We'll take the middle note (E) and move it down an octave (E C G). I've left the original E note in the chord grid on the right, so you can see where it was, but it's not played.

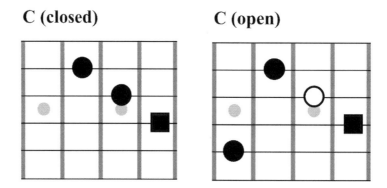

I call this voicing a "2 1" pattern, because we have two notes on adjacent strings, then we skip a string and have one note on its own. We can use the same shape to play C major triads across the neck like this:

Example 5a:

If we want, we can reorganise all of those voicings as "1 2" patterns: one note on its own, a string skip, then two adjacent notes.

Example 5b:

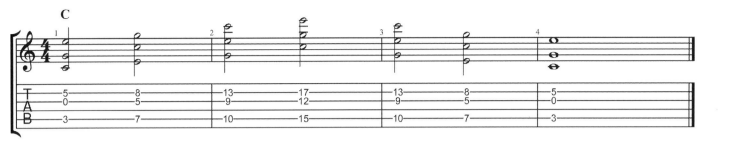

It's worth working on both fingering configurations and deciding which you prefer. Something I like to do is ascend with one pattern and descend with the other, to get a feel for which fingerings are easier. Here's that exercise with a C major on the top string set.

Example 5c:

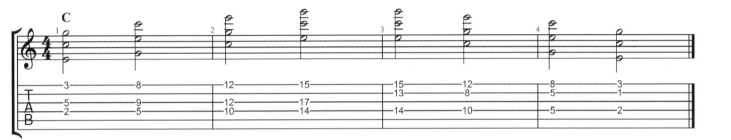

And, as you might expect, this can also be done on the lower string set too.

Example 5d:

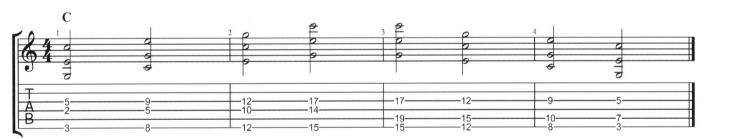

So far, we've only looked at things horizontally, but we can stay in position and work on vertical open voicings using our large barre shapes for reference. Here's a C major played vertically in all three shapes. Play around and experiment to see what fingerings you prefer.

Example 5e:

Just as we did with closed voiced triads, we can change notes in these open voicings to make major, minor, diminished or augmented sounds. I won't make you sit and work on all the diminished and augmented sounds because we'll be here all day, but minor triads are always useful. The following exercise works through alternate open voiced major and minor triads.

Example 5f:

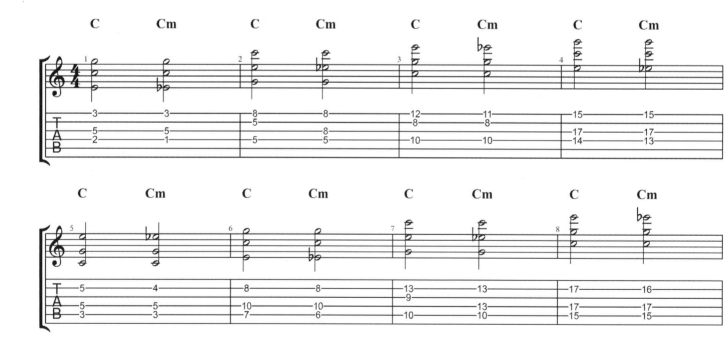

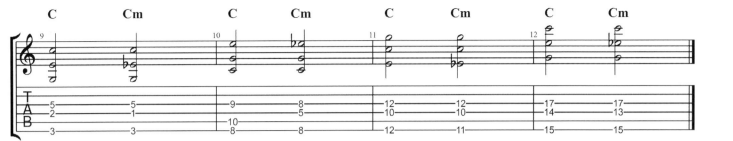

Here's a cool little chord progression inspired by the great Steve Morse. It uses both major and minor triads in open voicings and has an undeniable classical edge to it.

Example 5g:

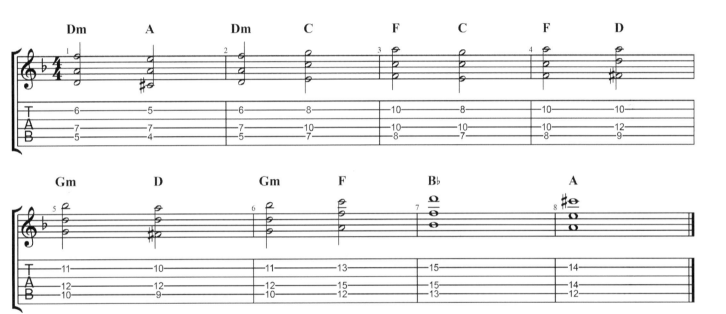

There's something different about that progression which we've not yet discussed: *inversions*.

If you've studied any music theory, you may have viewed our closed voiced triads as different inversions of the same chord. But you may also have noticed that I never once used that term.

An inversion simply means that you have a note other than the root of the chord in the bass. To me, the most important part of that description is "in the bass". We hear chords in context, in relation to a root note that we either imagine, or perhaps the bass or keys are playing. A C major triad played on the top three strings with E as the lowest note doesn't sound like an inversion, because we hear it in relation to the C harmony we're playing over. That's the reason why I don't really see those closed voiced triads as "inversions".

Look at the following example to understand my reasoning.

In bar one we have a closed C major triad with E as its lowest note. The bass on the audio track is playing a C root note, so it feels wrong to call this chord an inversion and label it C/E, because it isn't being played over an E note.

In bar two, we have a root position closed C major triad spelled (C E G). This time, however, the bass is playing an E underneath it. It doesn't matter that the guitar is not playing an inversion – it has been *made* an inversion because of the E bass note which gives it a specific sound.

In bars 3-5, I've moved to playing open voiced triads. The F/A chord definitely does sound like an inversion, especially when put in the context of F moving to F/A moving to Bb.

Example 5h:

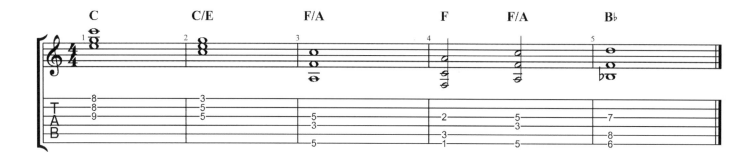

Now, if we revisited Example 5g, we could write out those chords more accurately as:

| Dm A/C# | Dm C/E | F C/E | F D/F# |

| Gm D/F# | Gm F/A | Bb | A |

What do all these inversions have in common?

They all have the 3rd of the chord in the bass. We call this "first inversion". First inversion chords have a powerful sound and feel quite "unstable". They are still major chords, but that bass note feels ready to move!

Notice in Example 5g that every time a first inversion chord is played, the bass note resolves up a semitone. Once you've played this movement a few times, you'll begin to hear it used all over the place.

The chorus of *Anyhow* by the Tedeschi Trucks Band is a good example of first inversion use. It uses an obvious E/G# that it sits on for a long time before resolving up to A.

Check out the following progression and see how the G/B chord always moves up to a C.

Example 5i:

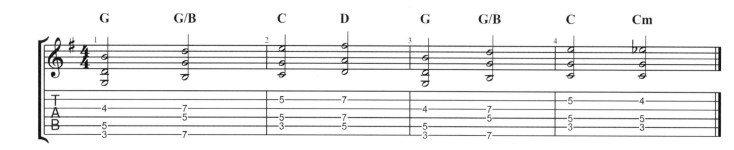

This is not the only way in which first inversions work though. Often you'll see inversions used that don't belong to the key. That's because they are also a great way to fill the gaps in a chord progression chromatically, but in a way that still logically ties the progression together. Maroon 5 use the following idea in one of their songs:

Example 5j:

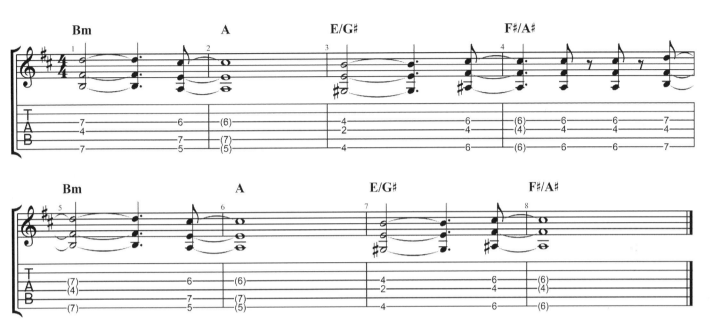

Inversions help to take us from one chord to the next and are used in classic songwriting all the time. Just ask someone like ABBA!

Example 5k:

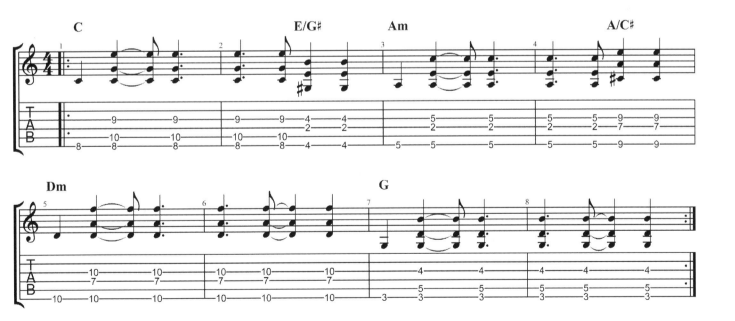

If we invert a chord by moving its 5th into the bass, we call that a "second inversion". These chords have a denser sound. They are not quite as stable as root position chords, but don't sound like they want to resolve in the same way as first inversion chords.

I think of the introduction to *Your Song* by Elton John for the sound of the second inversion. Here's that idea played in the key of G Major. In it we have a G chord followed by C/G. The 5th (G) of the C chord has been moved to the bass to create a second inversion, and it keeps that G bass note going throughout.

Example 5l:

It's worth noting that what we play on guitar will never supersede the bass player. They have the casting vote on how our chords are perceived by the audience. The inversions we play with different notes in the bass are nice ways to reinforce what the bass is doing. The previous example could, for example, be played using basic closed voiced triads, or open voiced ideas higher up the neck. They will have the same effect if the bass is holding down that G, like this:

Example 5m:

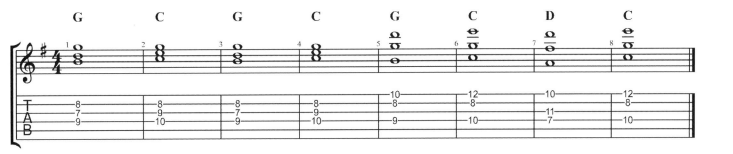

Here's one final example that combines open voiced triads and inversions to outline a longer chord progression.

Example 5n:

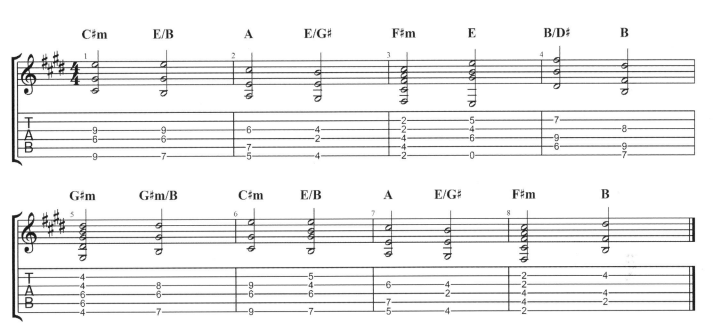

As I've mentioned, practice means taking an idea like open voicings and applying it to other concepts we've already studied – such as moving them around the Circle of 5ths, or simply applying them to any chord progression we know. The more we apply chords practically, the more they'll become part of our long-term, subconscious chord vocabulary. We just have to stick with them and put in the time.

Remember, the harder you're sweating while practicing, the more progress you're going to make. See you in the next routine!

Routine Six – 7th Chords & Triad Mutation

We've reached the halfway point in our chord routines and so far we've only talked about triads. That's because I genuinely believe they are *that* important to your personal development and study of harmony.

Moving on, we're going to talk about 7th chords. We'll look at the theory, how to construct them, and how we can apply them to the fretboard.

Using our tertian system of harmony, we built triads by stacking 3rds, using the 1st, 3rd and 5th degrees of the scale. If we continue that pattern and stack one more 3rd on top we have a 7th chord (1 3 5 7).

Technically, there are three different types of 7th we can add to a chord. The most common are the natural 7th of the major scale and the b7 of the natural minor scale. It's also possible to add a bb7 (yes, a double flat 7th!) which comes from the diminished scale, but we won't worry about that for now.

Before we play any chords, let's talk theory. We'll take the triads we know and add a 7th to each one, then see if we can name them. First, the major triad:

If we add a natural 7th to a major triad we get a major 7 chord. If we add a b7 we get a dominant 7 chord.

- 1 3 5 7 – Major 7

- 1 3 5 b7 – Dominant 7 (also just called a 7 chord)

Next, the minor triad. Add a b7 and we get a minor 7 chord. Add a natural 7th and we get a minor-major 7 chord.

- 1 b3 5 b7 – Minor 7

- 1 b3 5 7 – Min(Maj7)

It's also worth considering some other options.

Add a b7 to a diminished triad and we get a minor 7b5 chord (also called a half-diminished). Add a natural 7th and we get the very rare diminished major 7.

- 1 b3 b5 b7 – Min7b5

- 1 b3 b5 7 – DimMaj7

Finally, there's the augmented triad. Add a natural 7th to the augmented triad and we get a major 7#5 chord. Add a b7 and we get a dominant 7#5.

- 1 3 #5 7 – Maj7#5

- 1 3 #5 b7 – Dom7#5 (more commonly written as 7#5)

Spend some time committing these to memory, then we'll work on putting sounds to the names.

We'll start with what I call the *additive* approach. In other words, we'll play a triad then add a 7th on top of the chord. For example, we can take a C major triad and add a B note on top to give us a closed voiced Cmaj7.

Example 6a:

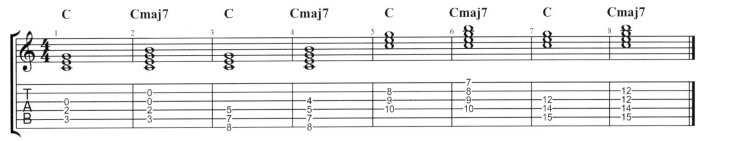

We can do the same using the C major triad but adding a b7 note, to give us the grittier sounding dominant 7 chord. Note that we can't achieve this in open position because we can't flatten the open B string.

Example 6b:

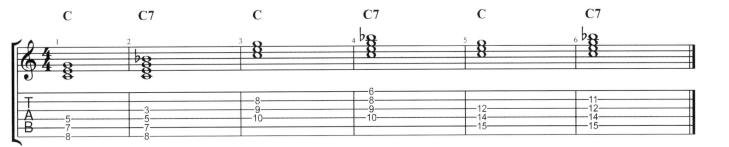

If we keep the b7 interval but lower the 3rds in all those chords, we convert them to Cm7.

Example 6c:

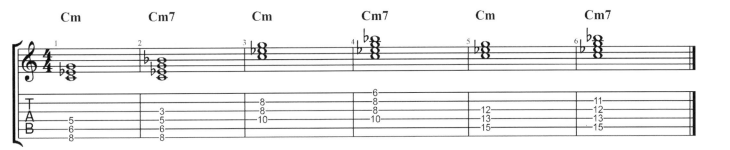

You'll notice that the more we delve into 7th chords, the harder it becomes on the hands. So it makes sense to have some standard grips for these 7th chords that we can pull out quickly to play songs. Below are the most common voicings for the most important 7th chord types. We'll discuss where they come from later – for now, we just need them under our fingers.

Example 6d:

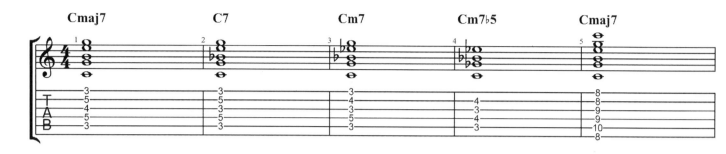

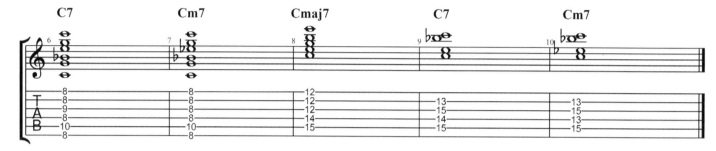

If we go back to our chord scales, we can quickly see where these 7th chords come from. When we harmonised the C Major scale into triads it produced:

C – Dm – Em – F – G – Am – Bdim – C

The C Major scale harmonised into 7th chords gives us all of the chord types in Example 6d.

Cmaj7 – Dm7 – Em7 – Fmaj7 – G7 – Am7 – Bm7b5 – Cmaj7

Notice that,

- All the minor triads (ii, iii, and vi) are now minor 7 chords

- Chords I and IV are now major 7 chords, but chord V is a dominant 7

- Chord vii is now a half-diminished or minor 7b5 chord

Using the first chord grip from the previous example, we can play the harmonised C Major scale like this:

Example 6e:

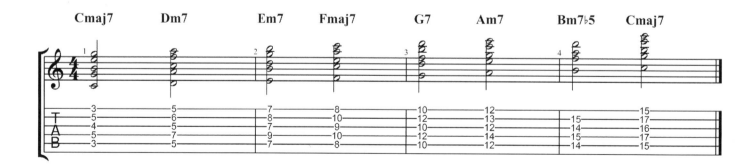

If we switch back to using closed voicings now, you'll suddenly see why having chord grips is a huge help for us. Here is the G Major chord scale played using closed voicings on the top strings. It's not easy!

Example 6f:

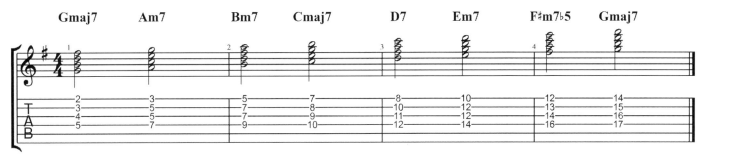

And what happens when we start to invert these chords? You'll quickly realise that it's impossible. Try the following idea, where I play the first Gmaj7 chord, then move each note up to the next note in the chord. Only pianists can play this stuff. We guitarists need a better solution!

Example 6g:

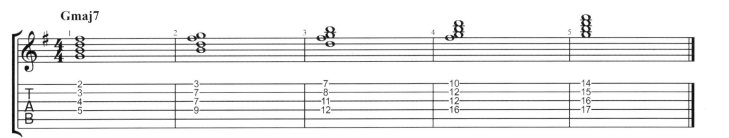

Clearly we need a different approach to practicing 7th chords – ideally one that's based on the triad knowledge we already have. This is where my "triad mutation" approach comes in!

The principle of this approach is to take a triad voicing and change one note for another to create the richer 7th chord sound we're looking for.

For example, we can take a C major triad and move the 5th interval up to the 7th. By doing that we change its 1 3 5 voicing (C E G) to a 1 3 7 voicing (C E B) which creates the sound of Cmaj7.

First have a listen to how this simple "mutation" sounds, then I'll explain why we can do it. Play it in all three of our triad positions, each time taking the 5th (G) and moving it to the 7th (B).

Example 6h:

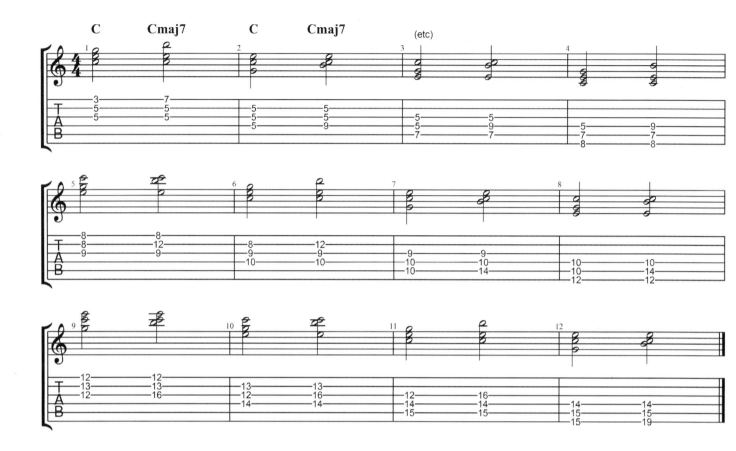

To know why this mutation works, we need to understand how each note in a 7th chord functions. Let's look at each interval and consider which are the really important ones and which ones could be sacrificed.

Root: this is the note we hear the chord in relation to. You might think it's important, but it's very likely that the bass/keys player will be playing this note, so we don't have to. Rootless chord voicings are very common in jazz.

3rd: this note is a key ingredient – it tells us whether the chord is major or minor.

5th: this note doesn't help us to identify the chord, it just makes the sound a little thicker. It can't tell us whether the chord is major, minor or dominant.

7th: like the 3rd, the 7th is the other important note that tells us the quality of the chord. For this reason, the 3rd and 7th of any chord are called the "guide tones".

When we mutated our C major 1 3 5 voicing to 1 3 7, we used the root and the two guide tones. Combined, they fully describe the sound of Cmaj7.

Some of the mutated voicings are more useful than others. Some just sound great and some are easier to play than others. We tend to gravitate towards the ones that suit our personal taste.

Now let's perform another mutation!

If we drop all those 7s down to b7s (1 3 b7) then we'll create a set of C7 voicings. These are all easier on the hands, but some still sound a little better than others.

Example 6i:

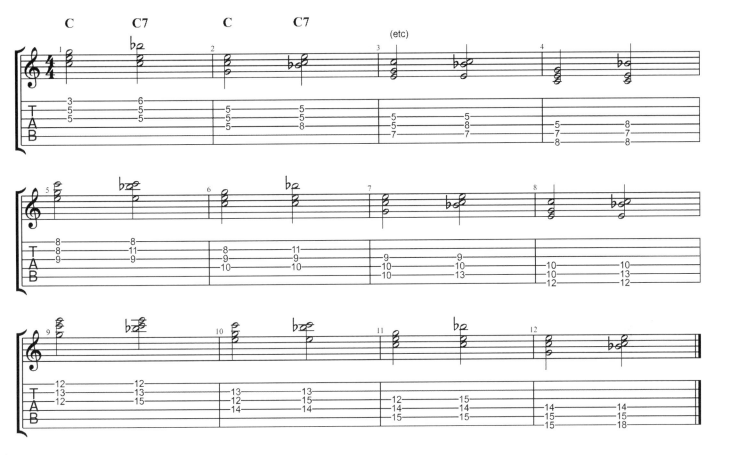

Let's mutate the voicings again. If we now lower all the 3rds in these voicings to b3s we'll have minor 7 chords. Importantly, these voicings will also work in place of minor 7b5s, because they don't contain a 5th.

Example 6j:

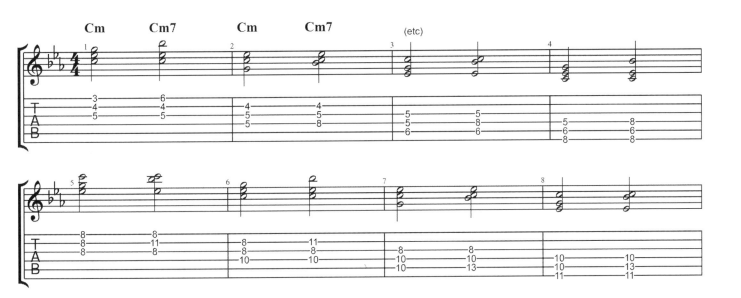

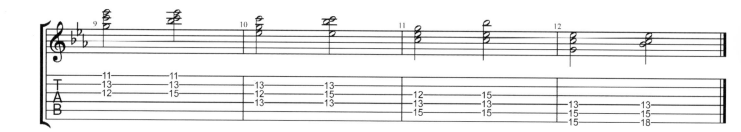

Let's take just ONE of these 1 3 7 voicings and use it to play a Bb Major chord scale. I don't want to scare you but there are 12 voicings. Played through all 12 keys that's 144 options! I won't write them all out here, but you can work on them in your practice sessions. Don't tell me you've run out of things to practice!!!

Example 6k:

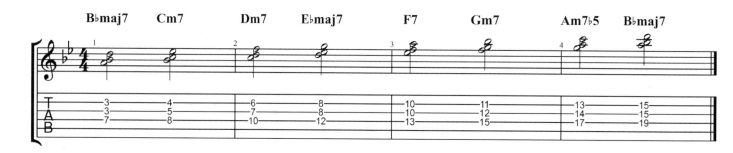

We've discovered that there are endless options available to us with 1 3 7 voicings, but we're only halfway in exploring triad mutations. There is another important one to consider! So far, we've created 7th chords by raising the 5th, but we can also mutate triads by lowering the 7th, so that 1 3 5 becomes 7 3 5.

Remember, our chord voicings don't need a root note – someone else is playing that!

We'll follow the same process as before, playing all twelve 1 3 5 triad voicings, lowering the root note each time to make 7 3 5 voicings. Let's do that now with C major – Cmaj7.

Example 6l:

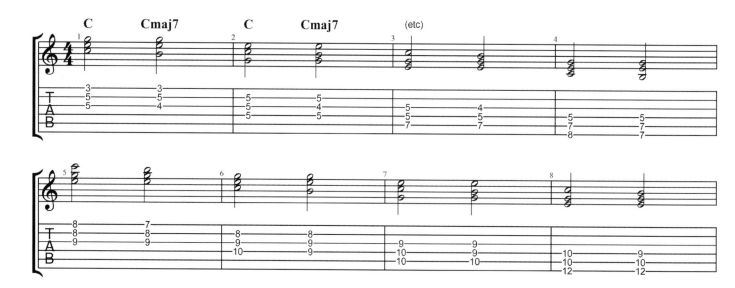

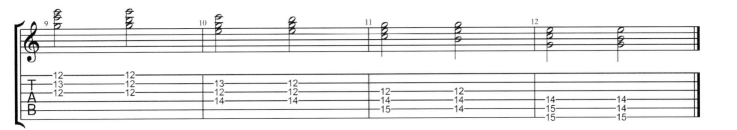

As we did before, let's now lower the 7ths to b7s to change the voicings to C7. If you recognise the sound, they are just the diminished triads you've been working on.

Example 6m:

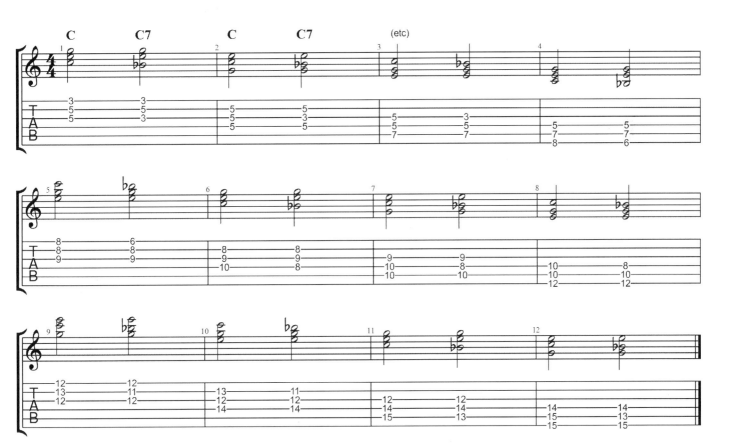

By lowering the 3rds to b3s we get to our minor 7 voicings. Do these look familiar? Yep, they are just Eb major triads! (NB: these minor 7 voicings won't work in place of minor 7b5s this time, because the chord contains the natural 5th).

Example 6n:

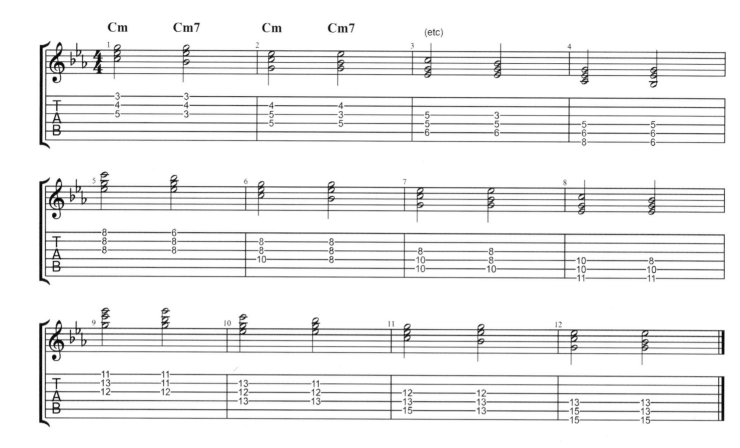

Now that we've completed our study of 1 3 7 and 7 3 5 shapes let's spend some time on musical context. I've said it 1,000 times and I'll keep saying it: I'm not a jazz musician, but I *think* like one.

That means I often use jazz standards for practice because they usually contain a lot of chord/key changes. So, to conclude this chapter, we'll look at the chords to the popular standard, *All of Me*.

I use the *Real Book* or an app like iReal Pro to reference the chord changes. A quick glance will show you that this tune is full of 7th chords. However, to begin with, we're going to ignore every 7th chord and just use major and minor triads to spell out the changes.

Example 6o:

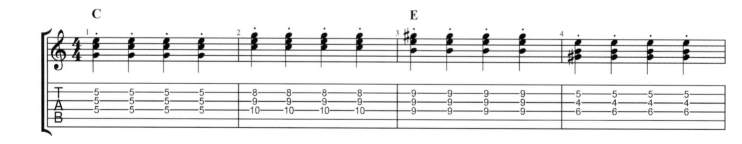

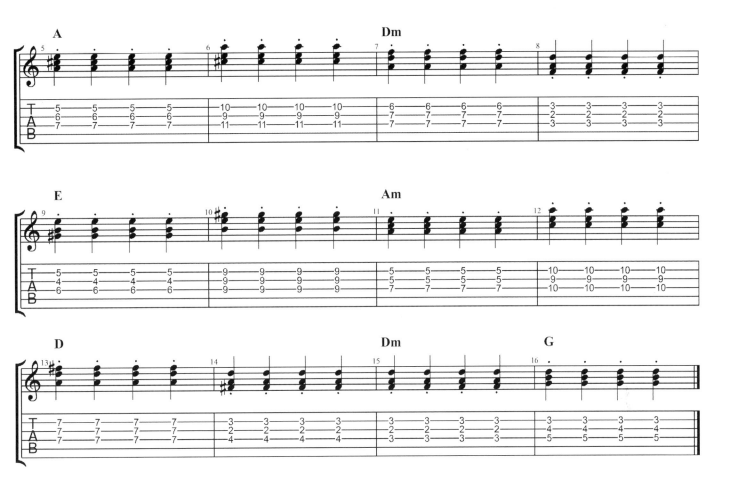

Using those same triads, I'll now turn them into 7th chords, either by lowering the root note or raising the 5th. Here's how it sounds.

Example 6p:

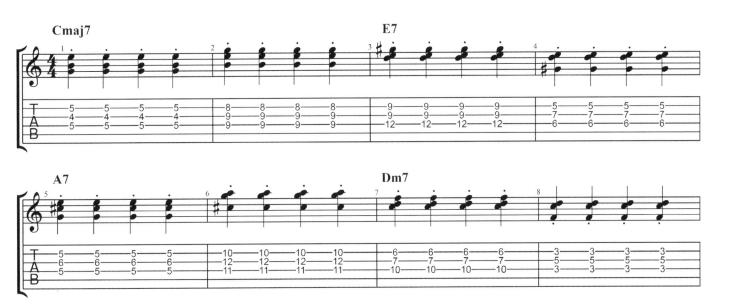

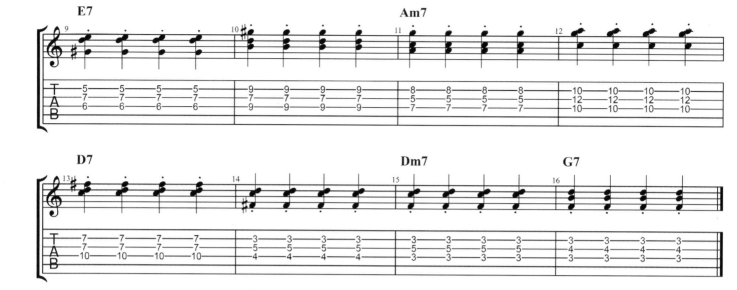

The sky is the limit here; we could also play it like this:

Example 6q:

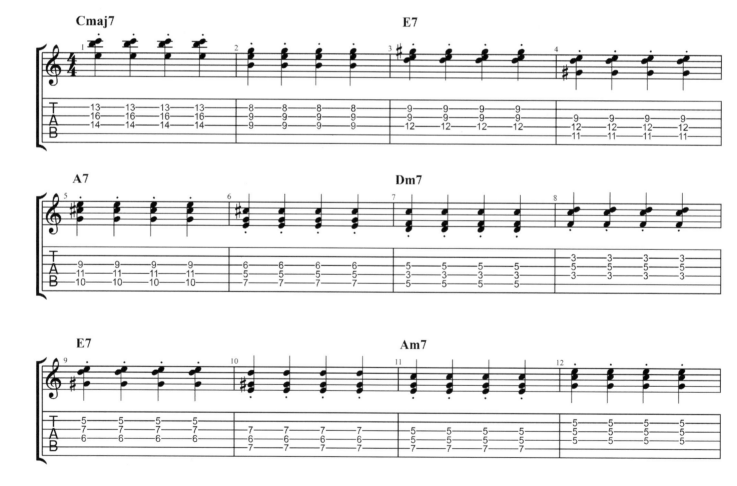

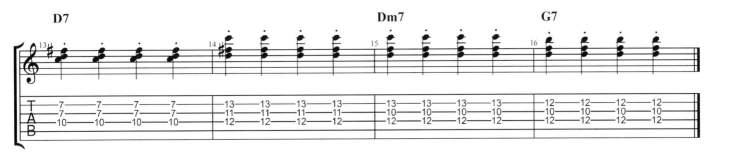

We have to remember that this book isn't just about learning, it's about practice, and about how *I* practice. We've looked at some of the possibilities on one tune, but there are countless others to work on.

By taking a song – even a random one you've never heard before – you are developing your brain's ability to work things out, rather than just memorise things. Playing the same song over and over quickly becomes an ineffective use of your practice time, so mixing things up is important. Try these other great jazz standards and work through them using the process we've established.

All The Things You Are

Polkadots And Moonbeams

Misty

Skylark

Stella By Starlight

All of these tunes have rich chord changes to work on, but we're just dipping our toe in the water. There are more songs out there than we can ever learn, so let's keep studying!

Routine Seven – Drop 2 Voicings

We've arrived at Routine Seven and we now know how to construct 7th chords, which are the most important intervals, and we have some tools for voicing them. However, the options at our fingertips thus far are a bit of a compromise.

Some of the chord grips omit notes, and we don't have good voicings for all chord types. The triad mutations are missing a note, and as soon as we begin inverting closed voiced 7th chords they quickly become unplayable. While all these chord options sound great and have their place, we still need a bit more flexibility – and this is where *drop voicings* come in.

Drop chords take closed voicings and spread them out in a way that creates a more open sound.

Remember when we took a C major triad (C E G) and dropped the middle note down an octave so that we had E C G?

That's all a drop voicing is!

There are various types and in this chapter we're looking at Drop 2 voicings.

A Drop 2 voicing takes a closed voiced chord and drops the *second note from the top* down an octave. Let's illustrate this with a Cmaj7 chord (C E G B).

In the Cmaj7 voicing below (left diagram), the second note from the top is G. So, we take that G and move it to the bottom (middle diagram).

However, the result is a voicing with a string skip, which can be hard to play, so we can reorganise the Drop 2 voicing to fit on adjacent strings (right diagram).

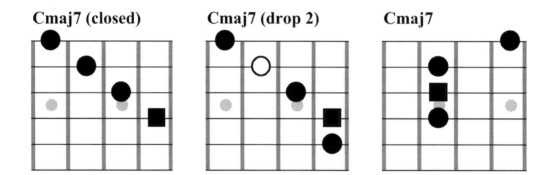

Rather than taking all four closed voiced major 7 chords, dropping down the second note from the top, then re-fingering them, it's much more efficient to take the reorganised Cmaj7 voicing on the right and move each note up to the next note in the chord. If we do that for Cmaj7, we get the following.

Example 7a:

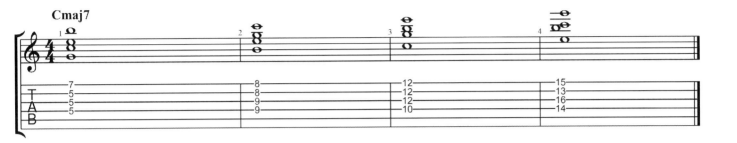

I think about these chords in terms of the note that is on top. This is our melody note. The first voicing is Drop 2 with the 7th of the chord on top. The next voicing has the root on top. The remaining two voicings have the 3rd and 5th respectively on top. Knowing this will help you down the road when you want to harmonise melodies with chords.

We can take these voicings and move them down to the two lower string sets too. Remember that as we introduce lower notes into our voicings, they start to sound like inversions. It's tough to find a place for voicings with the 7th in the bass when playing with other musicians, but that's not a reason to not know them.

Example 7b:

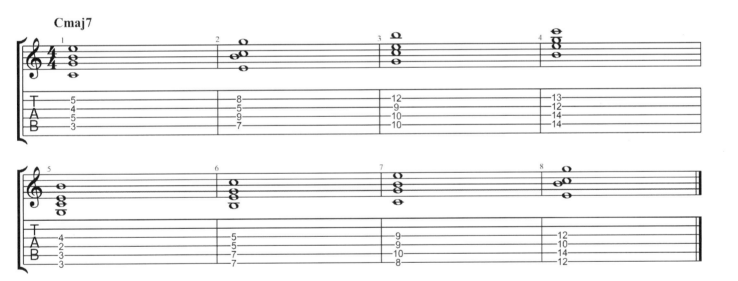

Let's play those voicings again but move them around the Circle of 5ths by going to the key of F.

Example 7c:

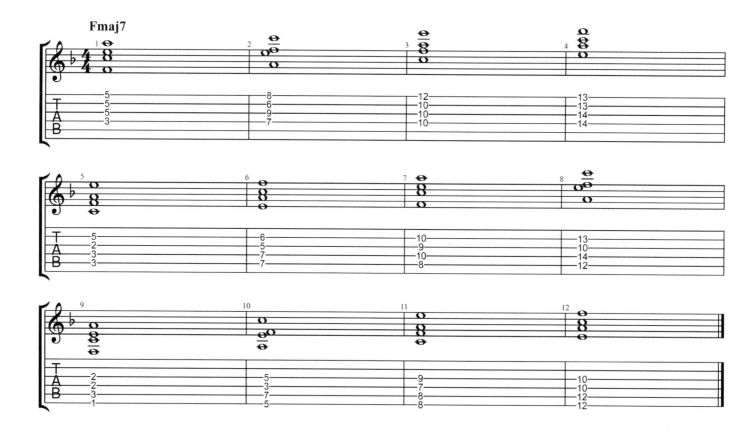

Now let's take those Fmaj7 voicings and turn them all into F7 chords by lowering the 7ths to b7s.

Example 7d:

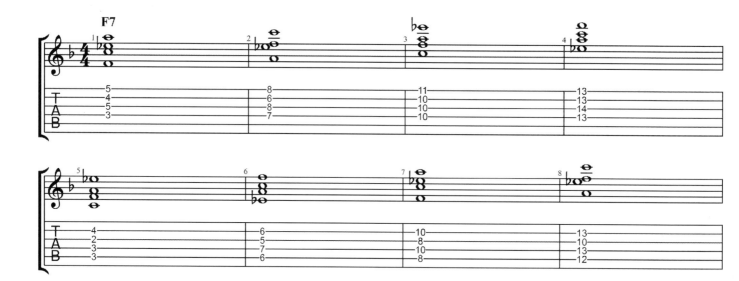

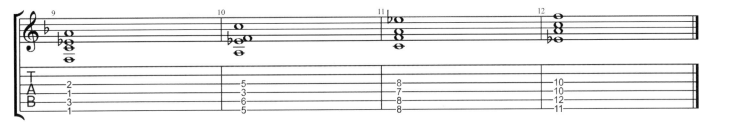

We're applying the same learning process here that we've followed throughout. Now we take those F7 voicings and move them around the circle to Bb. Being confident to play any of these voicings in any key is an essential part of chord mastery.

Example 7e:

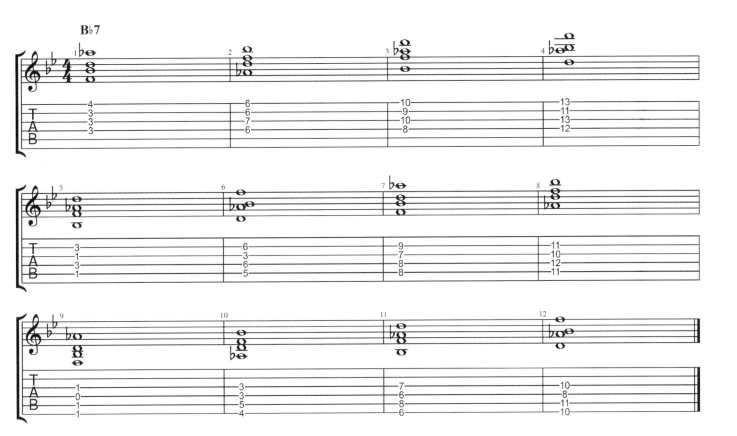

Now let's take those B7 chords and lower the 3rds to b3s to make Bbm7 chords.

Example 7f:

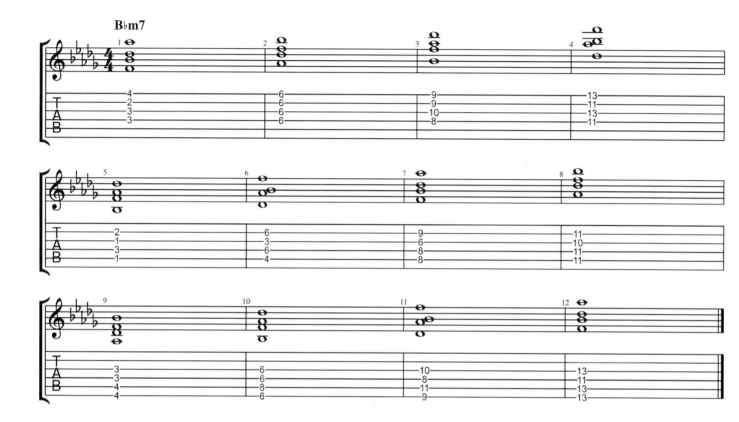

And if we move this around the circle again we end up playing Ebm7 voicings.

Example 7g:

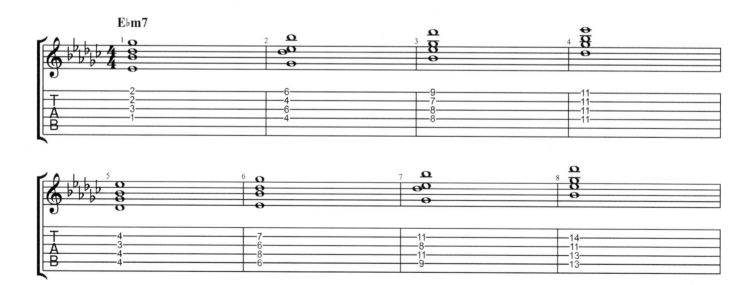

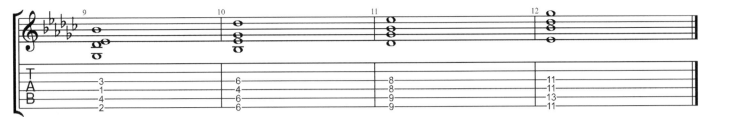

Hopefully, you can guess where we're going with this now! Let's lower all the 5ths to b5s to make Ebm7b5 voicings.

Example 7h:

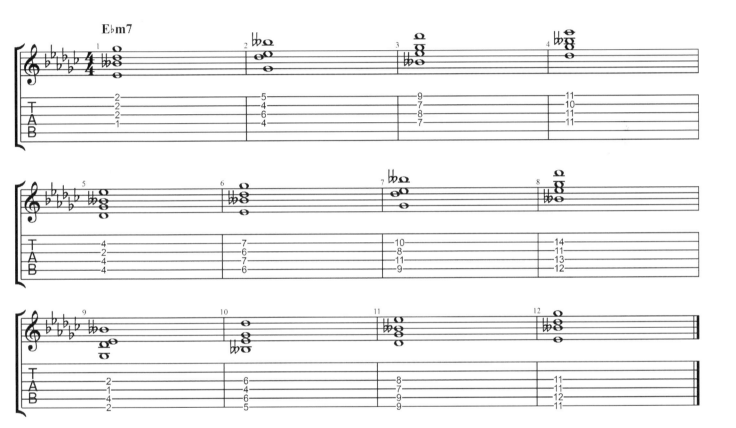

Using a Drop 2 chord to generate more voicings just opened up our options even more. Let's use this idea to play diatonic chord scales with different note intervals on top. You know the drill: you can practice these using all the possible voicings in all keys. I won't write them all out, but we'll do some of them.

First, an A Major chord scale played with the 7th on top.

Example 7i:

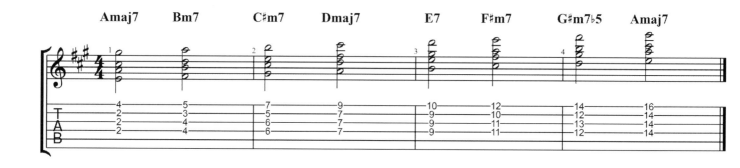

Here's C Major played with the 5th on top.

Example 7j:

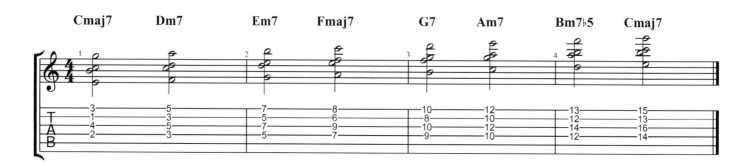

While there isn't a whole lot of use for drop voicings on the lowest string set, the middle set is viable. Here's a B Major chord scale played with the 3rd on top.

Example 7k:

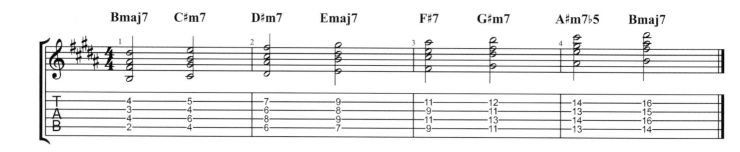

Let's apply what we've learned to a common chord progression: the major I–VI7–ii–V.

Astute readers will immediately look at this and think, "It should be I–vi–ii–V in a major key" and you'd be right, but a common change to the I–vi–ii–V (Cmaj7 – Am7 – Dm7 – G7) is to switch out the vi chord for a dominant 7 to give us Cmaj7 – A7 – Dm7 – G7.

This works on the principle of musical gravity. Dominant chords always want to resolve, and by changing Am7 to A7 (called the subdominant) we create a stronger resolution to the Dm7 chord.

Let's play those chords in position, first with the 7th on top, then the root, then the 3rd, then the 5th.

Example 7l:

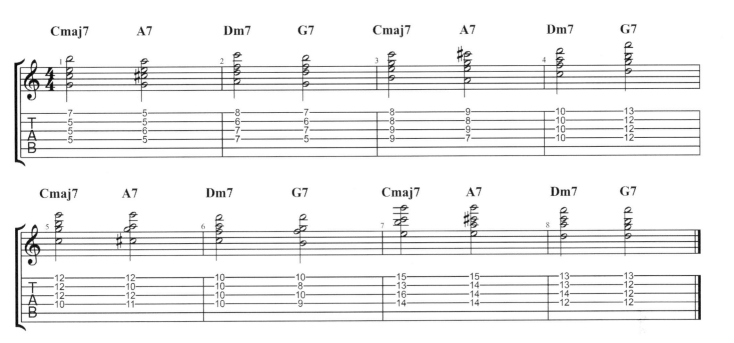

We can also work on this chord progression on the middle string set. First with the 3rd on top, then the 5th, then the 7th, then the root.

Example 7m:

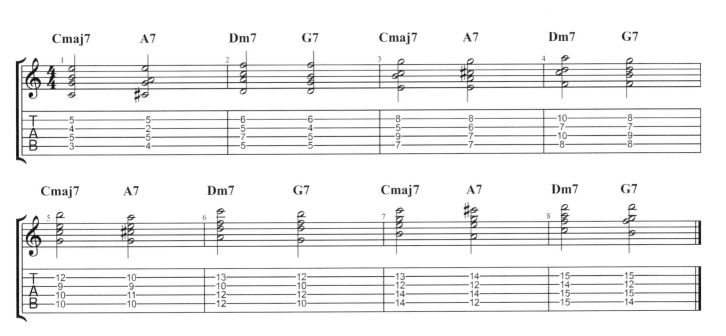

To conclude this routine, I want to give you one new chord type that sits adjacent to the chords we've learned so far. That's the diminished 7 chord and it has the formula:

1 b3 b5 bb7

Rather than learning it as an entity in its own right, it's better to adapt something we already know. It's tempting to think of taking a minor 7b5 voicing and moving the b7 down to a bb7, but there is an easier way. Instead, we take a dominant chord and raise the root a semitone.

The sharpened root becomes our new "1" interval and now we have the desired 1 b3 b5 bb7. Let's work this idea across the fretboard turning C7 chords into Dbdim7 voicings.

Example 7n:

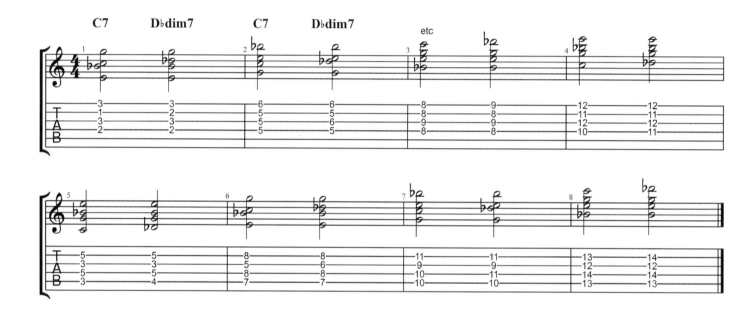

There is something very interesting about this idea. If we look at the diminished 7 chord in isolation, we realise that we can move *any* note in that chord down a semitone and it will create a *different* dominant 7 chord.

Practice the visualisation skill of playing a diminished 7 chord, lowering one of its notes a half step, then naming the dominant chord. It's a good workout!

Example 7o:

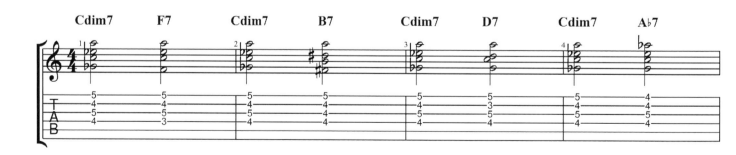

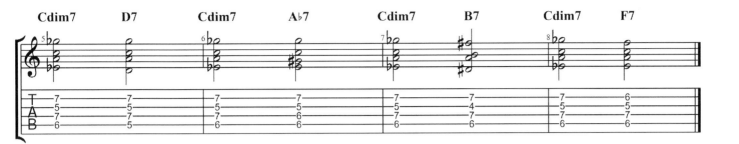

This chapter has been a good example of how a practice routine can generate much more than a week's work. You can spend a *lot* of time working these ideas through your playing, but as always, no rushing! You're only short-changing yourself if you skip ahead too quickly, so get to work on this stuff!

Routine Eight – Drop 3 & Beyond!

If you're still with me and have followed everything until this point, the title of this chapter shouldn't present a mystery. Here, we're going to look at Drop 3 voicings.

To create a Drop 3 we take the *third* note from the top in a closed voicing and drop it down an octave. Let's view this using the same diagram as the previous chapter.

Here, we take the E note of the chord and move it down an octave (middle diagram). Just like Drop 2 chords, it helps to have a consistent fingering system. Drop 2s were always played on four adjacent strings, but Drop 3 chords have a low note, a string skip, then three notes on adjacent strings (right diagram).

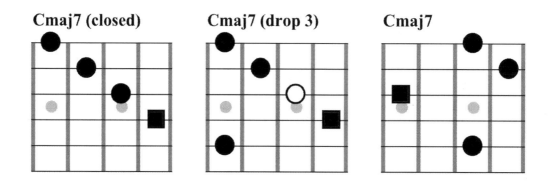

Drop 3 chords have a more open sound than Drop 2s. To my ears, Drop 2 voicings are piano-like, but drop 3s feel more guitar-centric.

When we spell out all the possibilities for Cmaj7, we have the following eight voicings.

Example 8a:

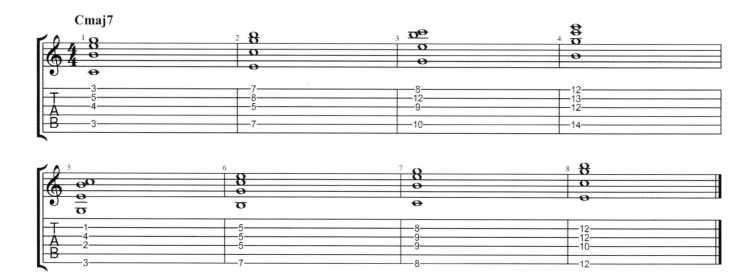

Practice until you have these voicings down. When you're comfortable with them, we can move onto other chord types. The first is the dominant 7.

Example 8b:

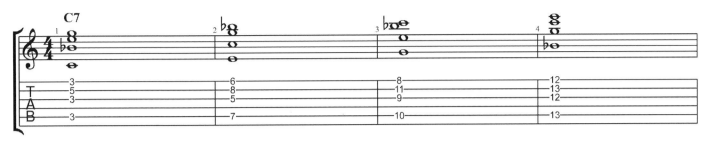

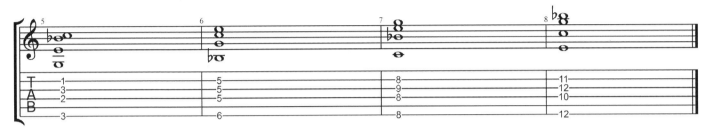

Let's make those voicings minor 7s by lowering the 3rds to b3s.

Example 8c:

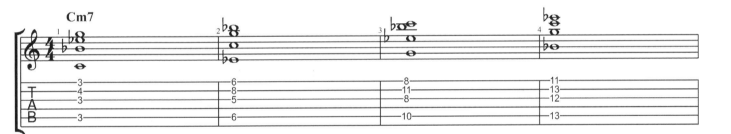

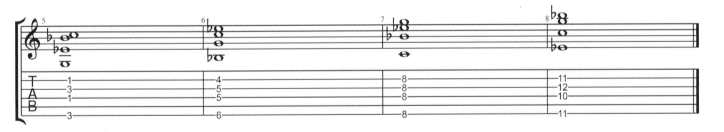

Then we can turn the minor 7s into minor 7b5s by lowering the 5ths to b5s.

Example 8d:

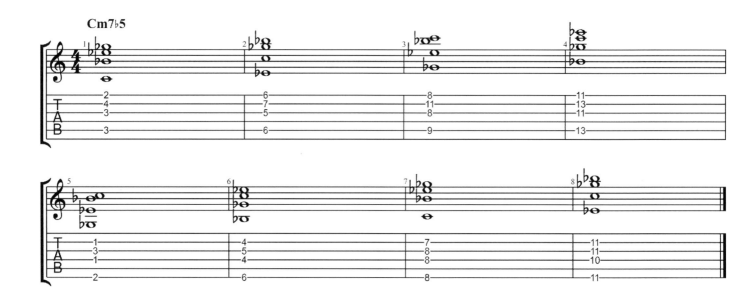

Now let's look at Drop 3 diminished 7 chords. In this arrangement, we can see just how symmetrical they are, with each voicing moving up three frets (a minor 3rd).

Example 8e:

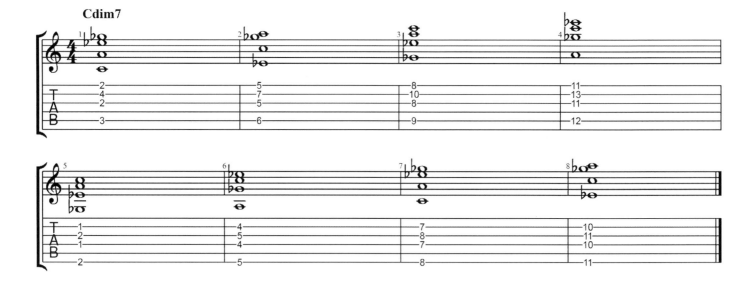

Now let's think of chord scales for a moment and play the most common Drop 3 voicing, with a root note on the low E string, through the G Major scale.

Example 8f:

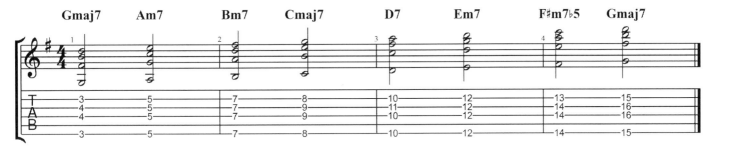

Now let's try an F Major chord scale, this time using first inversion voicings that move the 3rd to the bass. These Drop 3 chords do sound like inversions!

Example 8g:

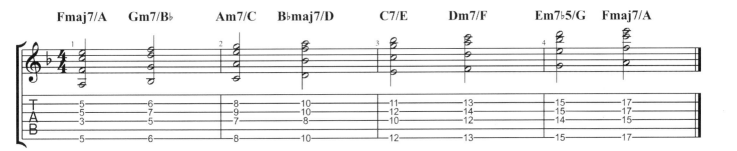

To test our comfort level with the drop chords we've learned so far, let's pause and use them to play through a Bird blues progression. We're going to limit ourselves to Drop 3 chords on the lowest string set (E D G B), and Drop 2 chords on the middle string set (A D G B).

Let's start with root position Drop 3 and 2 chords. We could call these our E and A shapes from earlier in the book.

Example 8h:

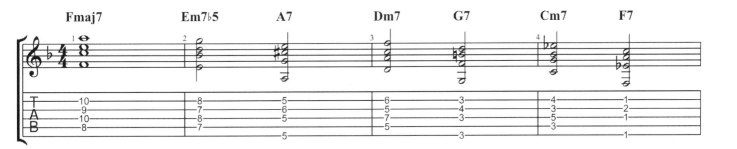

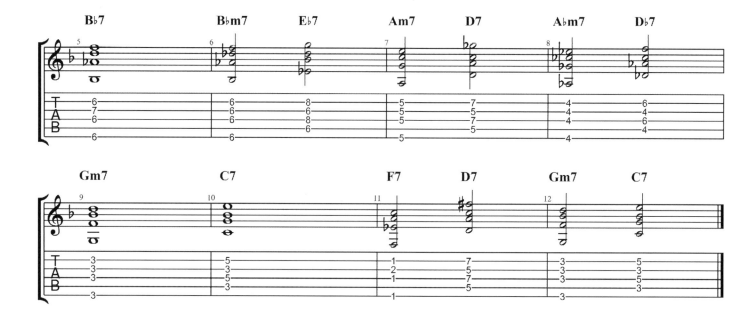

Here's a sunnier chord progression. Again, we're just limiting ourselves to the Drop 3 E shape and Drop 2 A shape.

Example 8i:

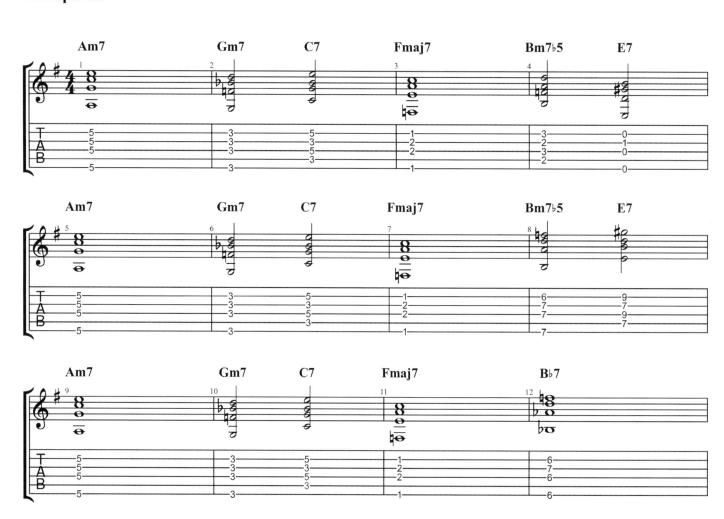

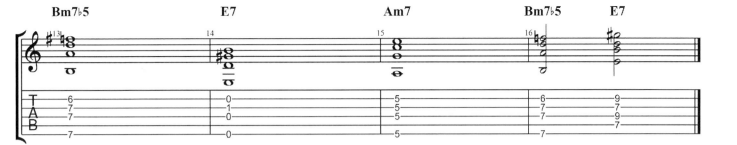

If we combine these voicings with our C shape closed voiced chords and grips, we can start developing some real flexibility when we play. I'm looking for my root notes, then sticking a chord voicing on top.

Example 8j:

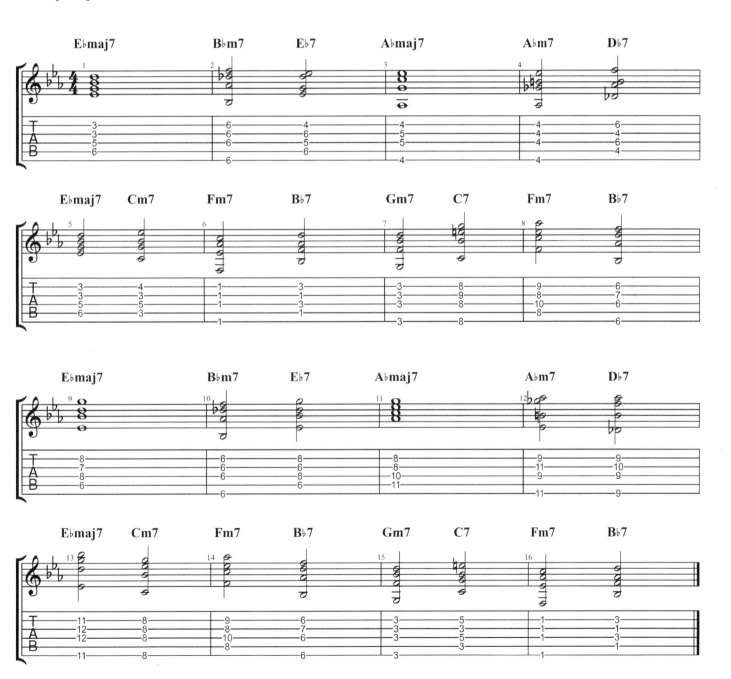

We've played through a few chord progressions using drop voicings, but to test yourself apply this idea to any progression/song you know. Growth is all about keeping your brain working, so keep on mixing things up. I don't want you to copy the same path that I've used, I want you to work out your own.

To close out this chapter, I want to put one more idea in front of you: the concept of Drop 2&4 voicings. As the name suggests, this is when we take a closed voiced chord and drop both the 2nd and 4th notes from the top down an octave. Let's return to our diagram to visualise it.

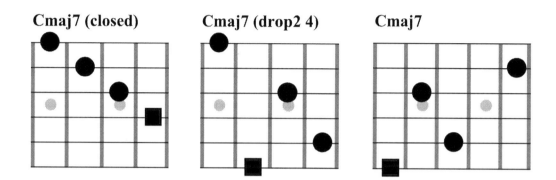

To organise these notes on the fretboard in a sensible way, I recommend playing two notes on adjacent strings, skipping a string, then playing two more adjacent notes, as in the right hand grid above.

These chords sound even more open than Drop 3 voicings and are a feature in the playing of many "out there" modern jazz/fusion icons such as Allan Holdsworth.

Here are Drop 2&4 voicings on the lowest string set for Cmaj7.

Example 8k:

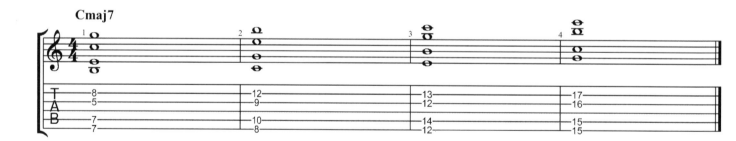

You'll probably notice that most of these voicings sound like they don't work too well. Why is that?

Well, a chord only needs to contain the right intervallic ingredients to be considered a chord, and the way in which we voice it has a big impact on how we hear it. These Drop 2&4 voicings sound like inversions. Plus, any chord voiced with its 7th in the bass on the low E string is going to sound muddy.

However, transfer them onto the top strings in the higher register and suddenly they're quite nice!

Example 8l:

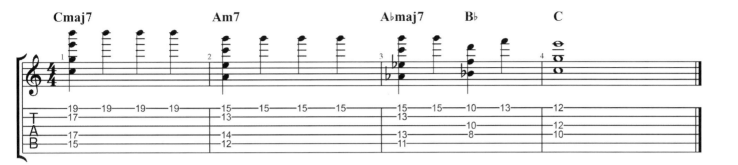

This throws up the topic of *voice leading*. The study of voicing chords and voice leading them (how we move from one chord to the next) is a lifetime's work and not something we can pursue here. There are some notable texts on the subject, like George Van Eps' *Harmonic Mechanisms* – three volumes clocking in at 900 pages! In other words, it's not something that can be mastered in ten weeks. However, as long as we focus on getting a little better each day, we're heading in the right direction.

Routine Nine – Chord Naming Rules & Extensions

I'll warn you up front: we're going to cover a lot in this routine and there will be a fair bit of theory amidst the examples! The most important aspect of this session will be learning about chord naming conventions. The reason we're looking at this is because I want to arm you to be able to interpret any chord symbol that is put in front of you in the future. So, when you see a Sus2 or Sus4 chord written on a chart, to give a simple example, you'll know exactly what it is and how to play it.

Let's start with triad naming rules.

From our studies, we know that triads contain variations of intervals 1, 3 and 5.

- 1 3 5 – Major
- 1 b3 5 – Minor
- 1 b3 b5 – Diminished
- 1 3 #5 – Augmented

We've talked about the function of these intervals. We hear a chord in relation to the root (1). The 3rd gives us information about the chord's quality (major or minor). The 5th just adds some density to the chord sound.

The first variation we should talk about is suspended chords. Suspended chords (usually written "sus") delay the commitment to a major or minor sound by switching out the 3rd for either the 2nd or 4th of the scale.

- 1 2 5 – Sus2
- 1 4 5 – Sus4

To play them, we can take any of our triads and move the 3rd up (to the 4th) or down (to the 2nd) to form a suspended chord.

Example 9a:

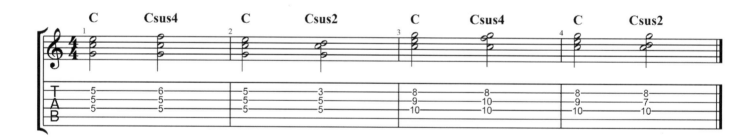

You should be able to play *any* of our twelve closed voiced triads and turn them into sus2 or sus4 voicings. I'm not going to write them all out here, because if you need them written out nine routines in, you need to go back for a refresher!

Sus chords are beautiful because they're so ambiguous in nature. They can be used to add inner voice movement to your chords for colour. One voicing I play a lot is the E shape triad on the D, G, B string set, and I'll hammer from the 2nd up to the 3rd.

If you want to get real serious with this chord, you can also add the root note on the low E string with your thumb! Here's me alternating between an Asus2 to A and Dsus2 to D.

Example 9b:

Sus chords are an example of where we change a note in a triad to turn it into something else, but we can also *add* notes to chords to create more colourful versions of the basic triad.

For instance, we can add the 2nd or 4th to a triad, and they are (aptly) called "add" chords.

The 2nd and 4th can also be called the 9th and 11th. They are the same pitches moved up an octave. So, common "add" chords are:

- 1 3 5 9 – add9 (sometimes called add2)
- 1 b3 5 9 – madd9 (minor add9)
- 1 3 4 5 – add11 (sometimes called add4)

There are lots of ways to play these chords, but not easily in the same octave, so we might omit some notes. The bass player will be covering the root, so we can, for example, move the root note up to the 2nd to create an add9 chord. Let's play A to Aadd9 now.

Example 9c:

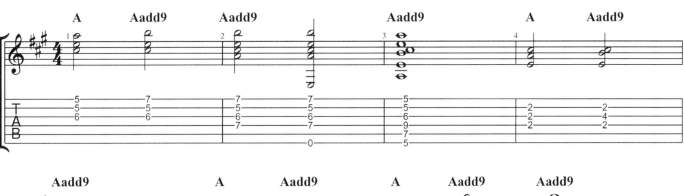

While the add11 is less common, these are beautiful chords if you can make the stretches. In order to play them, we'll take triads we know then drop the 5th down to the 4th. These chords work best when the 11th is higher up in the chord. We don't want it in the bass!

Example 9d:

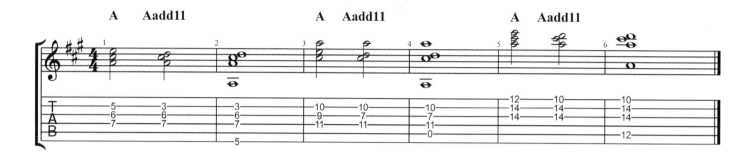

Now comes the 6th, a note added to triads so frequently that we stop saying "add"!

- 1 3 5 6 – Maj6

- 1 b3 5 6 – m6 (or min6)

Note that both of these chords have a major 6 (the 6th from the major scale). The minor 6 chord doesn't take the 6th from the minor scale.

These can be played as four-note voicings, but we can also play triads with the 5th moved up to the 6th. Here are some Maj6 voicings:

Example 9e:

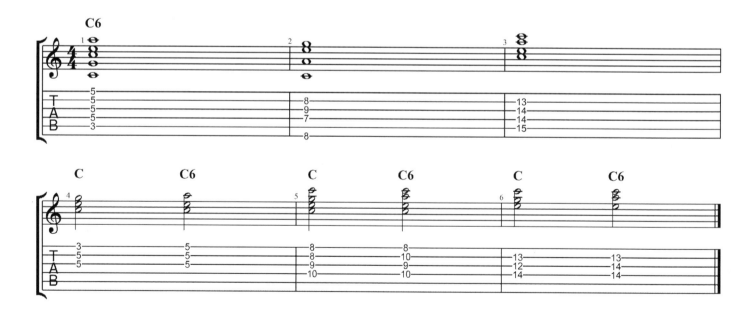

And here's our super cool minor 6 chord sounds. For these, we will raise the 5th up to the 6th, but also drop the root down to the 6th!

Example 9f:

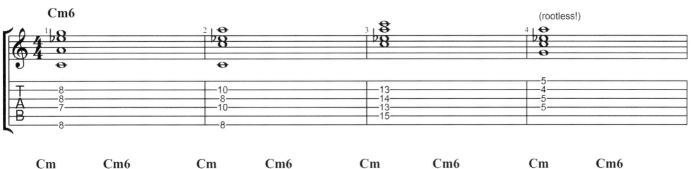

You might see combinations of 6th and 9th chords (written "6/9"), which are major chords with the 6th and 9th added:

- 1 3 5 6 9 – 6/9

It's rare that all five notes are played, so giving the listener the important notes (3rd, 6th and 9th) will do the job.

So, we've looked at adding more colourful notes to a triad, but what happens to the naming conventions when we add them to a 7th chord?

Let's take the 9th interval. We'll never see written Maj7add9. Occasionally I'll see Maj7(9) written with the added note in brackets but I don't like that. I prefer to see Maj9. To cite another example, nobody needs to see C7(9, 11, 13) when C13 will do.

We name a chord according to its highest extension. Maj9 implies we've taken a major 7 chord and added the 9th to it. If it simply said "add9" we'd know it was a triad-based chord.

When we see a Maj11 chord, it's implied that 9th is already in the chord. If we see a Maj13, it's implied that both the 9th and 11th are in the chord.

Let's briefly note the construction of major and minor 9th chords then play them.

- 1 3 5 7 9 – Maj9

- 1 3 5 b7 9 – 9

- 1 b3 5 b7 9 – m9

- 1 b3 5 b7 9 – m9b5

When you play these voicings, you should be able to stop and list off each interval in the chord in relation to the root note. If you can't, pause and take some time to do that.

Example 9g:

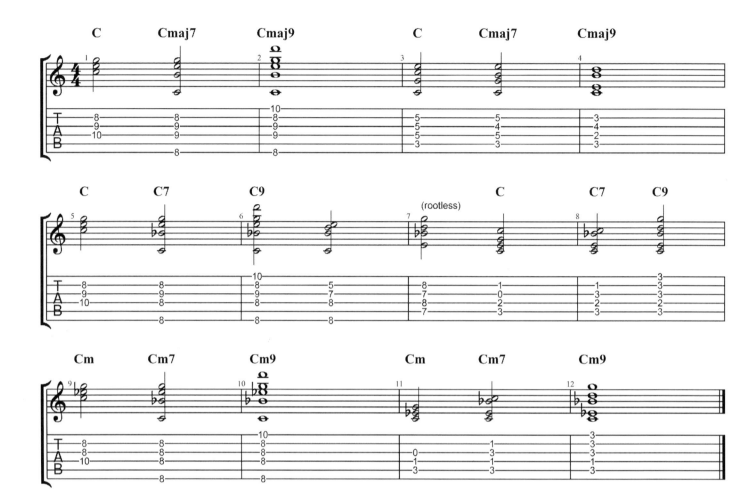

The 11th interval doesn't sound good on a major 7 chord, so it's often left out, but it works on dominant and minor chords.

- 1 3 5 b7 9 11 – 11

- 1 b3 5 b7 9 11 – m11

13s follow all the same rules.

- 1 3 5 7 9 13 – Maj13

- 1 3 5 b7 9 11 13 – 13

- 1 b3 5 b7 9 11 13 – m13

Occasionally, you'll see a 7th chord that contains the 11th but not the 3rd. What do we call that? It has a suspended quality, but still has the 7th, so "7sus" does the trick. Sometimes you'll see "9sus" chords too.

Example 9h:

We've covered almost all of the intervals you're likely to come across. All that's left are the alterations we can make to dominant chords: the b9, #9, b5/#11 and #5.

Let's start with the #9 because it's the ever-popular "Hendrix chord".

- 1 3 5 b7 #9 – 7#9

In fact, any of these intervals can be added to a dominant chord in any combination to make an altered dominant:

- 1 3 5 b7 b9 – 7b9

- 1 3 #5 b7 – 7#5

- 1 3 #5 b7 #9 – 7#5#9

- 1 3 #5 b7 b9 – 7#5b9

And there's nothing to stop us combining natural and altered extensions, such as:

- 1 3 5 b7 b9 13 – 13b9

- 1 3 #5 b7 9 – 9#5

The key to using these intervals is to know where they sit around your E and A shapes. Then you'll be able to add them without thought. Each one has its own flavour, but they all add tension and want to resolve like a standard dominant 7 chord.

Here are some altered dominant chords in the key of F Major. We're playing C7alt in the E shape.

Example 9i:

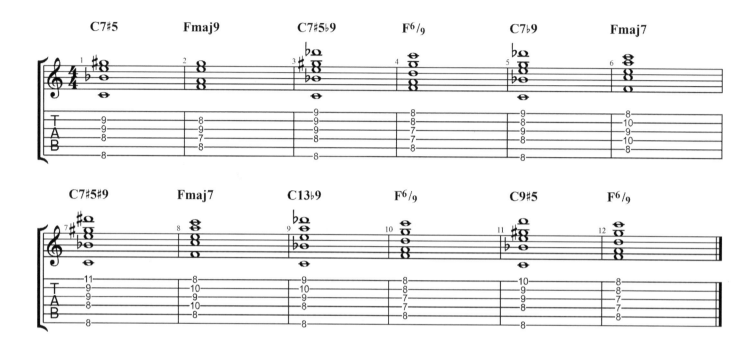

Here are some more altered dominants, now in the key of C with G7alt in the A shape.

Example 9j:

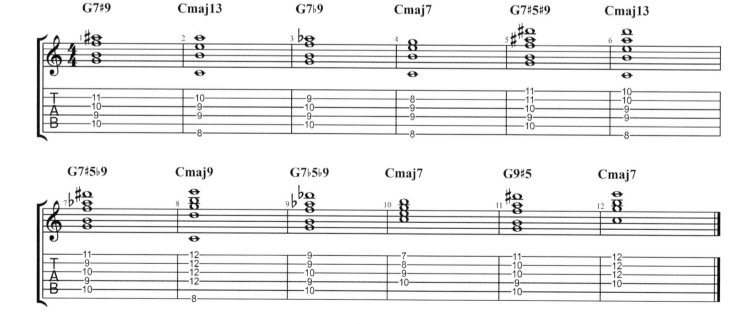

These alterations aren't commonly found on chords other than dominant 7s, with the exception of the #11 on major 7 chords. This makes sense because the 11th interval on a major 7 chord is incredibly sour! Raising it a semitone adds a nice, mysterious sound. And we can add natural extensions too:

1 3 5 7 #11 – Maj7#11

1 3 5 7 9 #11 – Maj9#11

1 3 5 7 9 #11 13 – Maj13#11

These chords work great either as the IV chord in a key (where they are diatonic) or as a bit of a surprise on a I chord.

Example 9k:

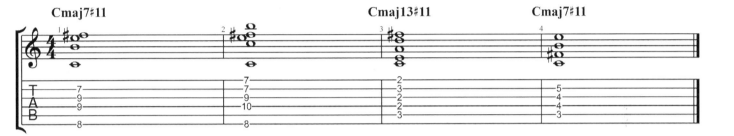

Experimentation is the key to becoming confident using chords like these. I don't get out my theory book when I want to play them, I just put them in chord progressions and see what sounds work.

One of the best ways to experiment with them is to play chromatic melodies on the top of our chords. This forces us to use extended and altered chords to find the melody note we're looking for.

For example, I'll take a ii–V–I progression in C Major (Dm7 – G7 – Cmaj7) and add a descending chromatic line on top.

I might play a Dm9 for the ii chord with the E on top. Then the E note needs to drop down a semitone to D# over the G7 chord, so it has to be a G7#5. Then the D# will drop down to D, so the I chord has to be a Cmaj9.

Here's that done with a descending chromatic line on the B then E string.

Example 9l:

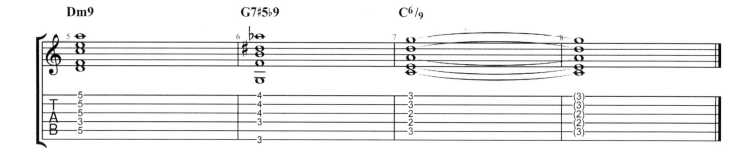

You could do the same with an ascending chromatic line too.

Example 9m:

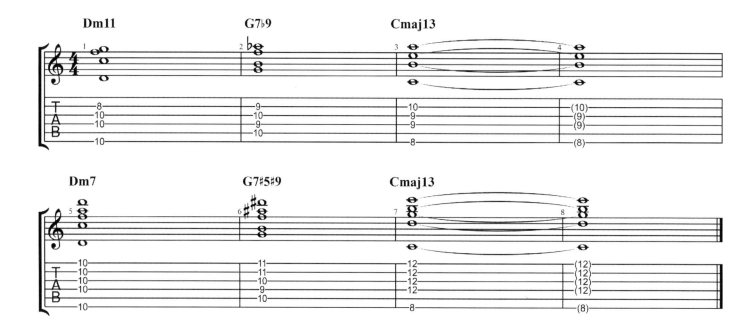

If we jump back to look at one of our previous chord progressions, we can try out some of these extended chords in place of vanilla 7th chords.

There is an element of focusing on the melody notes for these chords, but essentially I'm just having fun adding different extensions to see what I like and what I don't. In a practice routine, I'd sit and come up with many different ways to get through this progression.

Example 9n:

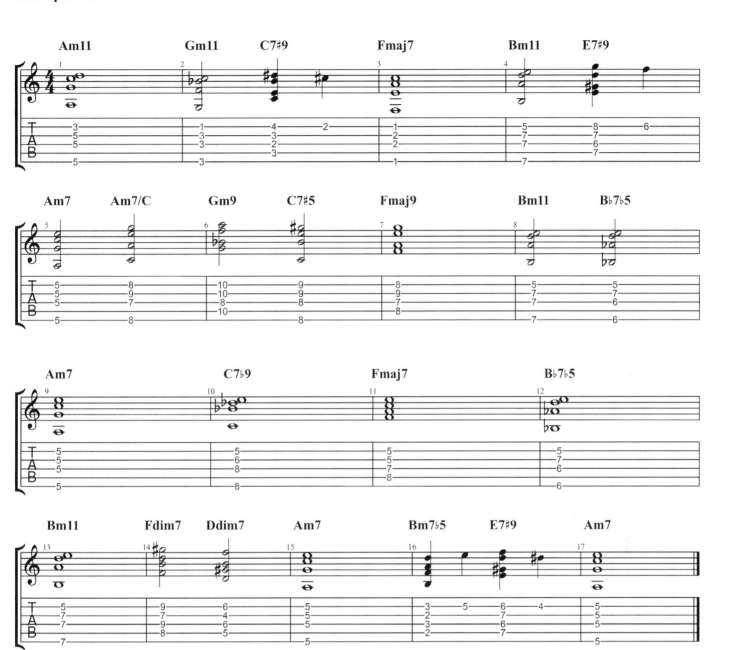

And, when I'm done with that, I'll pull up other progressions and work my way through those – jazz standards, RnB tunes, soul – it doesn't matter. Time spent thinking about and experimenting with harmony will always help develop our minds and ears, so dig deep, and I'll see you for the final routine!

Routine Ten – Slash Chords

If you thought the last routine was a lot of work, I have some good and bad news…

The good news is, this is the last routine! The bad news is, this one will have you thinking the most by a long shot. However, don't be afraid to focus on small ideas and keep revisiting this routine. I wanted to include this chapter to get you thinking about, and experimenting with, harmony on a deeper level.

You've probably heard the term "slash chord" and seen chords written down like G/B or F/G. The chord names contain a slash, so they're slash chords! Most often they mean a chord played over a specific bass note. E.g., G/B means a G triad played over a B bass note.

You might think, "Sure, we saw that chord when we looked at inversions" and you'd be both right and wrong. Technically, an inversion is a form of slash chord, but that's not what people mean when they refer to slash chords. Usually, they are written on chord charts because a chord is being played over an unexpected bass note.

We've learned that we hear chords in relation to the bass note. We can play a beautiful sounding C major triad (C E G), but the bass player holds all the power. And if the bass note changes to a note that's not in the chord, such as Bb, suddenly our chord doesn't sound like C major anymore. We hear chords from the bottom up, not the top down.

Let's take that exact scenario. At this point, to figure out what's happening in the harmony, we have to analyse our C major triad in the light of the new Bb bass note. Bb effectively becomes our new "1" so…

- C is the 2nd over Bb

- E is the #4 over Bb

- G is the 6th over Bb

Expressed as a formula, this new chord is 1 2 #4 6.

It's tricky to name this chord. There is a 2nd instead of a 3rd, so it's a sus sound. There is no 7th to tell us whether it's major, dominant or minor, but there is a #4 which suggests a Lydian chord. Here are a few ways we can play it:

Example 10a:

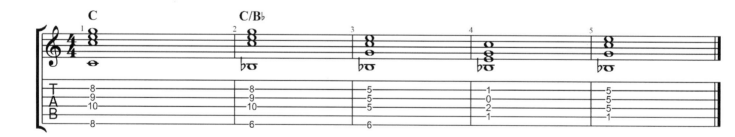

That's one slash chord, but we can put *any* triad over *any* bass note. In fact, we don't have to limit ourselves to triads, we can add alternative bass notes to 7th chords too. The question is, what works and what doesn't? And where do we start?

We need a system in place to help us "audition" and process this stuff in a comprehensive manner, and that's where my *chromatic superimposition* exercise comes in.

The idea is simple: we take a triad and play it over all twelve chromatic bass notes. Then we make a note of the intervals that are created. Finally, we try playing each chord and name the results (if possible).

You can do this just sitting with your guitar. Play a C major triad on the D, G, B strings with a C root under it, and work out the intervals visually. Then, shift the bass note up a semitone and repeat the process, working out the intervals in relation to the new root note, and so on.

Or, to make the process easier, write it all down. I've completed the exercise for the C major triad and put the results in the table below. The triad notes appear across the top, and every chromatic note is listed down the left-hand column. So, we can see, for example, that if we put an F bass note under the C triad, the F becomes the new 1, the C note is now the 5th, E is the 7th and G is the 2nd. The result is an Fma7sus chord.

Bass Note	C	E	G	Chord Name
C	1	3	5	Maj
C#/Db	7	b3/#2	b5/#4	
D	b7	2	4	7sus
D#/Eb	6	b2	3	
E	b6/#5	1	b3/#2	(inversion)
F	5	7	2	Maj7sus
F#/Gb	b5/#4	b7	b2	7alt
G	4	6	1	(inversion)
G#/Ab	3	b6/#5	7	Maj7#5
A	b3/#2	5	b7	m7
A#/Bb	2	b5/#4	6	Lydian/Maj13#11
B	b2	4	b6/#5	(inversion)

When it comes to naming these chords, we'll often be able to view them in a few ways. We might take a few liberties and sometimes the description will be helpful and sometimes not! The really important thing is to take note of the voicings you feel are usable and remember how to find them.

There are a couple in the above table that I'd want to know.

7sus – major triad played from the b7.

Maj7sus – major triad played from the 5th.

m7 – major triad played from the b3.

Maj7#11 – major triad played from the 2nd.

The only way to test these out is to immediately apply them to a simple chord progression. Let's go with a ii–V–I in C Major (Dm7 – G7 – Cmaj7) and let's focus on viewing each chord as a triad over a bass note.

For the Dm7 I'll play Dm7, which can also be viewed as an F major triad over D. F is the b3 of Dm7.

For the G7 I'll play G7sus. This can be seen as an F major triad over G – F/G.

For the Cmaj7 I'll make it a Maj7sus. That's a G major triad over C. G is the 5th – G/C.

Another option for Cmaj7 is the colourful Cmaj13#11. That's a D major triad over C. D is the 2nd – D/C.

Have a listen to how these ideas sound.

Example 10b:

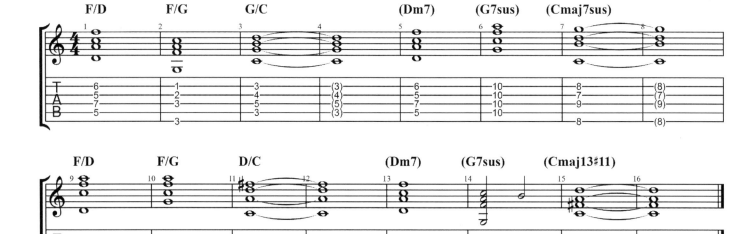

The most valuable thing you can do with voicings you like is to slot them into chord progressions. From that list, the 7sus is the most useful one to me. I use it all the time in chord progressions in place of a V moving to a I, as it's a little softer than the classic V–I sound. This is so common it's often written as IV/V.

Here's a chord progression where I've switched out the two dominant chords for 7sus sounds. Eb/F in place of F7 and Bb/C in place of C7.

Example 10c:

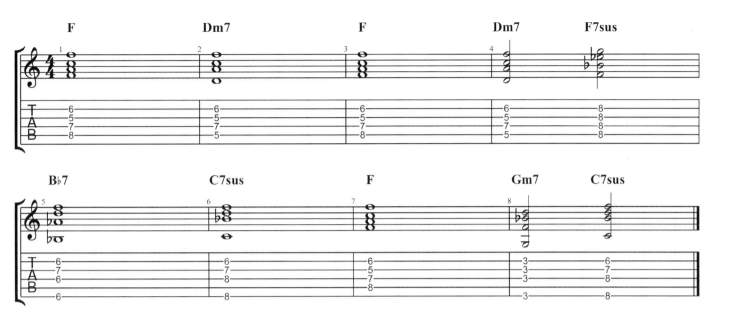

We've done the *chromatic superimposition* exercise with a major triad, but we can do it with a minor triad too. Here is the table of results for a C minor triad.

Bass Note	C	Eb	G	Chord Name
C	1	b3	5	min
C#/Db	7	2	b5/#4	
D	b7	b2	4	
D#/Eb	6	1	3	(inversion)
E	b6/#5	7	b3/#2	
F	5	b7	2	7sus
F#/Gb	b5/#4	6	b2	
G	4	b6/#5	1	(inversion)
G#/Ab	3	5	7	Maj7
A	b3/#2	b5/#4	b7	m7b5
A#/Bb	2	4	6	6sus
B	b2	3	b6/#5	

I like all of the named chords here. The 7sus as a minor triad from the 5th is a nice alternative to the major triad from the b7. Here's an example where I combine the two, also using a minor 7 built from the 3rd to make a major 7 chord.

Example 10d:

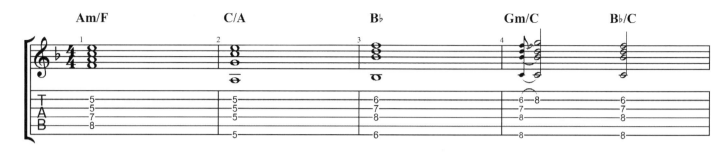

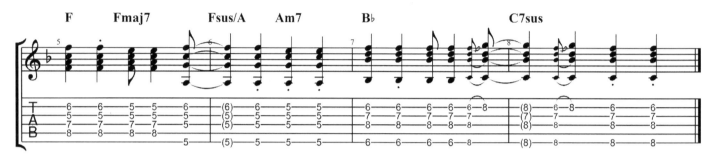

Another great use of these minor triads is alternating between the I and ii over a major chord/bass note. Over a C root note, I could alternate between C major and D minor triads. The C will sound like a major triad, while Dm/C gives us a suspended sound. It's a nice little shift from an inside sound to a more colourful sound and back.

Example 10e:

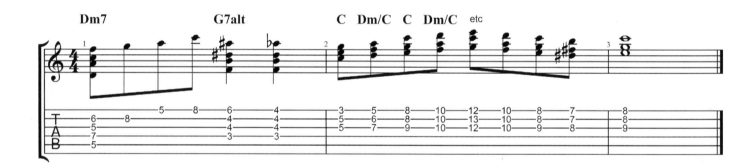

I want you to get on board with the idea of chromatic superimposition and the process of working it all out! Draw up a table, work through it, then do another one the next day. I've done this countless times and each time I get a bit quicker at it. It really helps to embed the useful note relationships.

For example, from my study of chromatic superimposition I know that playing an augmented triad from the 5th of a chord will give me a beautiful min(Maj7) sound.

First, I'll play the slash chords with bass notes, then I'll just play the triads and let the bass guitar deal with the bass notes. In the real world, that's how I'm using this stuff. We work with the bass to create the sound we want.

Example 10f:

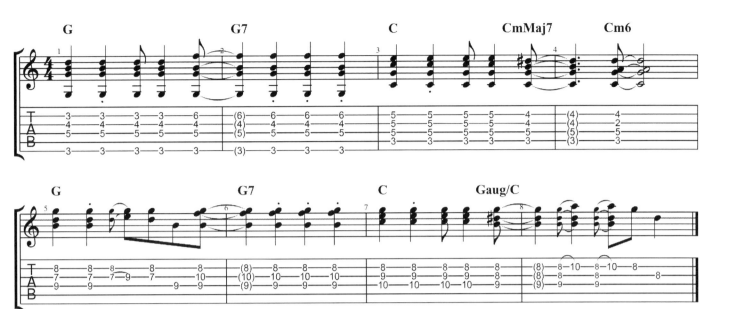

I won't make tables for diminished and augmented chords – it's over to you to work through that process. Instead, I want us to look at 7th chords because there is so much rich harmony to be found when we start with four notes rather than three. Below is a chromatic superimposition table for major 7 chords.

Bass Note	C	E	G	B	Chord Name
C	1	3	5	7	Maj7
C#/Db	7	b3/#2	b5/#4	b7	
D	b7	2	4	6	13sus
D#/Eb	6	b2	3	b6/#5	
E	b6/#5	1	b3/#2	5	(inversion)
F	5	7	2	b5/#4	Maj9#11(no 3rd)
F#/Gb	b5/#4	b7	b2	4	
G	4	6	1	3	(inversion)
G#/Ab	3	b6/#5	7	b3/#2	
A	b3/#2	5	b7	2	m9
A#/Bb	2	b5/#4	6	b2	
B	b2	4	b6/#5	1	

Because major 7 chords have more notes in them to begin with, it can be hard to voice them with different bass notes, but here are some that work well:

- C13sus (Bbmaj7/C)

- Cmaj9#11 (Gmaj7/C)

- Cm9 (Ebmaj7/C)

Example 10g:

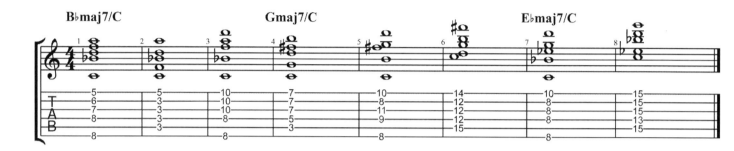

The skill in the application of this idea is knowing where you can place a major 7 voicing in order to create one of these richer sounds. For example, to turn a Dm7 into Dm9 we can play a major 7 from the b3, a.k.a. Fmaj7/D.

Example 10h:

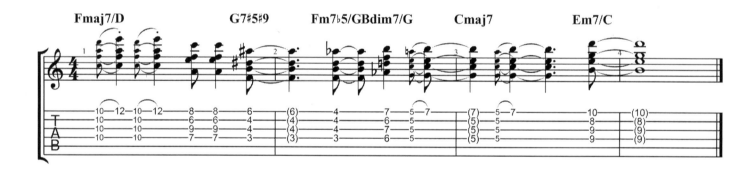

In the previous example, we also had slash chords with minor 7 and minor 7b5 sounds played over different bass notes, so let's look at those briefly. Here's the table for C minor 7.

Bass Note	C	Eb	G	Bb	Chord Name
C	1	b3/#2	5	b7	m7
C#/Db	7	2	b5/#4	6	
D	b7	b2	4	b6/#5	
D#/Eb	6	1	3	5	6
E	b6/#5	7	b3/#2	b5/#4	(inversion)
F	5	b7	2	4	11sus
F#/Gb	b5/#4	6	b2	3	
G	4	b6/#5	1	b3/#2	(inversion)
G#/Ab	3	5	7	2	Maj9
A	b3/#2	b5/#4	b7	b2	
A#/Bb	2	4	6	1	sus
B	b2	3	b6/#5	7	

All of the named slash chords are usable sounds. I particularly like that 11sus sound and use it over dominant 7 chords, which I'll then shift into an altered voicing to create a nice bit of tension.

Example 10i:

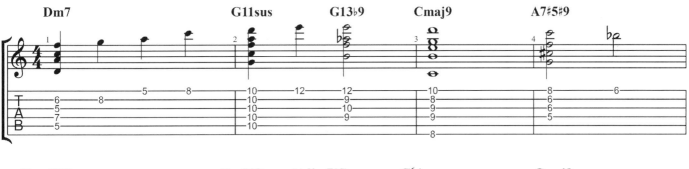

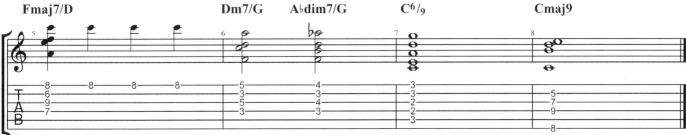

There aren't as many applications for the dominant 7 chord, because it's such a strong sound on its own, but before moving on I'd still encourage you to draw out a chart and work on the skill of identifying the intervals and trying to name the chords.

The minor 7b5 chord is a little more useful.

Bass Note	C	Eb	Gb	Bb	Chord Name
C	1	b3/#2	b5/#4	b7	m7b5
C#/Db	7	2	4	6	Maj13sus
D	b7	b2	3	b6/#5	7#5b9
D#/Eb	6	1	b3/#2	5	(inversion) – m6
E	b6/#5	7	2	b5/#4	
F	5	b7	b2	4	Sus4b9
F#/Gb	b5/#4	6	1	3	(inversion)
G	4	b6/#5	7	b3/#2	
G#/Ab	3	5	b7	2	9
A	b3/#2	b5/#4	6	b2	
A#/Bb	2	4	b6/#5	1	
B	b2	3	5	7	

Here's a blues that combines minor 7b5 voicings with different bass notes.

Example 10j:

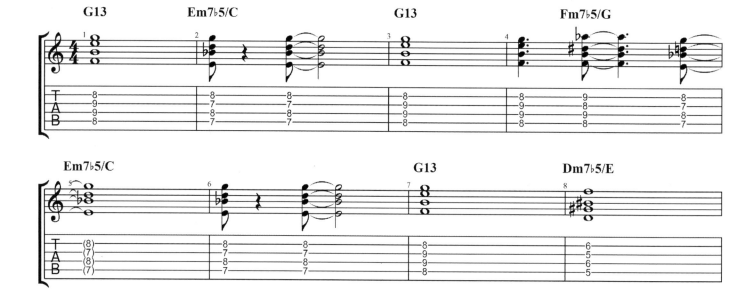

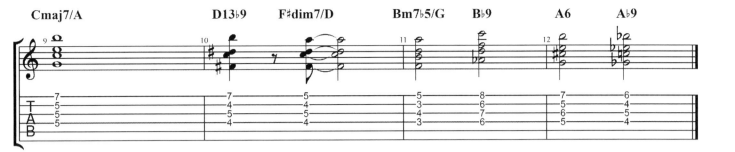

Finally, here's an example that makes use of the interchangeability of minor 6 and minor 7b5 sounds, which are essentially just inversions of each other. The IV chord (F) moving to a iv6 (Fm) is a nice sound in itself, but if we play the latter as a slash chord we can create a richer harmony.

Dm7b5 has the same notes as Fm6. If we superimpose that over a G bass note, we get the beautiful sus4b9 sound you'll hear in the music of the great Stevie Wonder. You can only really discover ideas like this through harmonic exploration!

Example 10k:

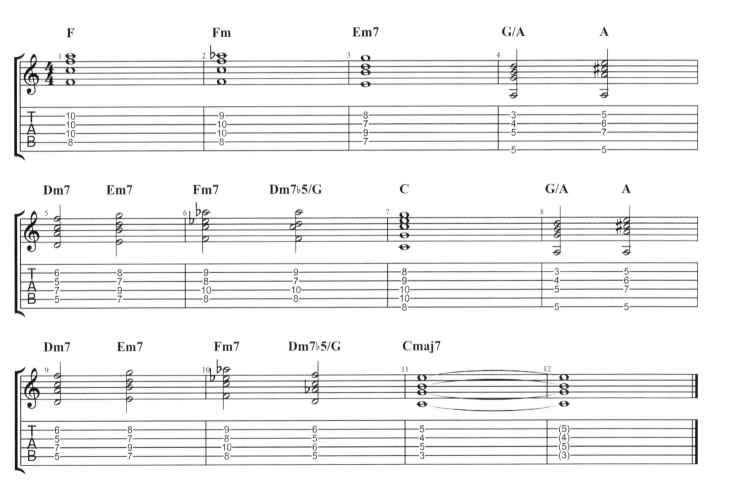

Work on this idea on your own for all possible 7th chords. When I was at university, we did this exercise for all the common 7th chord types, then moved onto more exotic chords such as Maj7#5, 7b5 and a bunch of others that felt like busy work! What this process achieved was to expand my ears to new sounds, and it gave me the ability to pick out sounds that I couldn't hear before. (Like the ending of John Coltrane's *Naima*, where he goes from an Abmaj7/Eb to Gmaj7#5/Eb!)

The more you dig into harmonically rich music the more you'll discover wild chords like these. Only now, you'll be better equipped to decode and play them. This isn't a week's work, of course, it's a lifetime's journey, but week by week you can learn new sounds and, in time, they'll become as familiar to you as a major chord.

Conclusion

Well, that got in depth pretty quickly!

Hopefully, you are now in a position to confidently build any chord that you see on a chart, and have a better idea of how to name any chord that you find on your guitar.

This book has laid an important foundation for us before we move on to look at arpeggios in the next book – because arpeggios are all about using chord sounds in a linear fashion to create melodies. Without the knowledge of what the chord is, what it sounds like, and why we play it, an arpeggio won't make any sense.

With this study under your belt, you should be shifting your perspective to think in a more *vertical* manner about chords, and be able to consider how the things you play are impacted by the bass note you're playing over, and how that changes what the listener hears.

Ultimately, music is near infinite. There are so many approaches to harmony and plenty of music out there that contains rich sounds. I mentioned Stevie Wonder, who is a huge influence on me, but anything that has a jazz influence is going to require a deeper understanding of harmony and an ear for hearing it.

Whether it's Michael Brecker's work with the Brecker Brothers, or Scott Henderson with Tribal Tech, many musicians have explored the concepts we've looked at with wonderful results. The more you learn about harmony, the further you can delve into the world of music and find things you'll be better equipped to understand.

I hope you enjoy your new-found understanding of harmony, and that it lights a fire of excitement under you. I trust that it will serve you as well as it has served me.

Good luck!

Levi